The 7 Deadly Threats To Your Recruitment/Search Firm In The New Economy & How To Avoid Them

Terry Edwards

The 7 Deadly Threats To Your Recruitment/ Search Firm In The New Economy & How To Avoid Them

Testimonials

"Happy to say that I have won business from putting Terry's methods into practice so I have no hesitation in recommending him to non-competitors especially if they are in a different geographical location!"

Richard Blann
RandKA Flexible Recruitment Solutions

"Terry has an engaging style and a unique outside-the-box approach to recruiting methodologies which I appreciate. Continually being open to new ideas, communication styles  *and techniques related to our business is important given the ever-changing climate of the business environment."*

Joe S. Murawski
Focused Hire

 *"I have been recruiting for nearly 10 years. When I was first approached by Terry Edwards I must confess I just couldn't imagine that you could get recruitment business without cold calling. You see, in all my recruiting career 'cold calling' and 'word of mouth' was the only way I was able to get business. That has all changed since working with Terry. There are two main benefits our business have got from working with Terry. The first one is, it has opened my eyes to the other effective methods of getting more clients. And secondly, in one week alone we generated 40 sales leads without making a single cold call. If you are serious about growing your recruitment business, I would recommend Terry Edwards."*

Jim Foster
Antal international Network

"If not for your insight and inspiration I would not have had the courage and motivation to make the changes I have to improve my marketing and business strategies.  *We have changed our website to have a call to action, have a proactive marketing strategy that is consistent and producing results, numerous clips on you tube that talk about who we are, a vision about recruiting that allows us to stay true to who we are, we don't need to be everything to every client we just need to be the best at who we are. You are not always right but dead on more than any other recruitment coach and advisor I have found in 20 years."*

Jeff Abram
SearchWest Inc.

 *"I have owned my own recruitment firm for 14 years now, and I must say I was reluctant to engage drewcoaching as I questioned if I would get my monies worth, also I believed that if there is anything that needs doing to improve the performance of the business then I would do it. However what I have found with working with drewcoaching is, I am more focused than at any other time in my career, it is also great to have a sounding board to vent some of my frustration that comes with running a recruitment business. The main advantage of engaging drewcoaching is my marketing knowledge has increased substantially and our sales have improved dramatically. If you are looking to increase sales and performance of your team I would recommend drewcoaching..."*

Eloise Shelton
Vanilla Recruitment

"I've been in business for over 17 years. Out of everything Terry has shared with me, I found the "permission marketing" aspects most useful. Terry shared with me the attraction marketing process that encourages my potential clients to come to me, rather than me always having to chase them. I would recommend Terry to any Recruitment/Search Firm Owner who wanted to know more about marketing and attracting clients."

Curtis Baer
Barrington Search Group

"Terry has provided me with some very thought provoking comments and fresh ideas. Happy to recommend Terry's marketing advice and tips to other Recruitment Business owners who want more ideas around attracting clients."

Max Roberts
Walbrook Search

"We have been in business for 12 years. We specialize in placing marketing/digital marketing candidates in luxury categories including beauty and wine & spirits. Terry has provided me with some very helpful tips on attracting clients and increasing profits. I would definitely refer Terry to another recruiting firm who wanted to grow their business."

Jan Liscio
Patrickson-Hirsch Associates

"As a company, "Russells" have been in business for nine years. However, I worked for two other companies previously and have been around the Recruitment Industry for over 25 years. Terry seems to know exactly how difficult our market place is and knows all the pitfalls we come across on a day to day basis. In an industry notorious for it's secrecy, it's good to hear from someone who knows how you feel. We would be delighted to endorse Terry wherever we can."

Marge Russell
Russell Recruitment

"We've just finished our year end and have exceeded our STRETCHED target. (We beat our original target by 24% and our stretched target by 3%). Additionally we have raised  *the proportion of retained business from virtually nothing to about 50%, we have changed the structure of the business and have Business Development Consultants and Delivery Consultants (Resourcers) which makes us more effective. And finally (you will be proud of me), we are doing our first LIVE seminar at the NEC, to existing, old and potential new customers."*

Jon Salt
Affinity Search

 *"Terry, your clear step by step plans for generating leads, regardless of the delivery method is the number 1 most useful thing I am learning from you. Creative information that forces me to re-think business. It lifts the horse blinders in a sense!*

Your ability to connect with top performers and outline their successful processes is useful and it's great to be reminded to 'take action'...

Content generation is useful, and other lessons on how to appeal to our client base. I believe the "profit club" will be a useful addition as a gathering place for your materials that can be accessed anytime by your customers. I would certainly recommend you to non-competing firms."

Dave Drohan
Bridge Point Search

"I have been a recruitment business owner for 16 years and although I recognised the value of coaching I had a number of reservations about working with drewcoaching. I was  concerned that as they are UK based and I am in Ireland, they may not be in touch with the economic and business nuances here. I also had reservations about the time I would need to commit with an already very busy work life. I have been working with drewcoaching for 6 months now and none of my initial reservations have held true. I am really enjoying the coaching process and the value it is bringing to my business. It's great to have an independent person who is interested and invested in the success of my business and who really understands the strategies, methods and techniques they are sharing with me as they have real business experience with them. It has also been reassuring to know that I am not going 'mad' on occasion and that my challenges are all fixable and changeable. I have been given the steps to take action and implement the changes needed to succeed. Even when the necessary changes have been quite difficult, drewcoaching have provided support and insight, which has increased my confidence in the actions across many aspects of managing my business. The practical aspect of their coaching around systems and process has *been invaluable. Over the past six weeks since beginning to implement some of the structure and procedures into some areas of our recruitment process that were proving particularly challenging, we have had a great month in terms of revenue, which I directly attribute to the recent work I have been doing with drewcoaching. I wouldn't hesitate to recommend drewcoaching to any recruitment business not in competition with me. For any business that is, I would rather keep them a secret.."*

Mark Markey
The Recruitment Bureau

"I have been a recruitment business owner for 15 years and in that time I have met numerous coaches and trainers. I wasn't keen at first to work with drewcoaching as I  *thought after nearly 15 years in the business there was little else I could learn about building a recruitment business, another concern was the fact I would be sharing my companies details with someone who works with many of my competitors Since working with drewcoaching, I have experienced an amazing transformation in business development. As a business we are able to generate more sales enquiries than ever in the history of the business and all of them without ever making a cold call. In fact we generated 82 leads in 4 days and signed one retained assignment, which when you consider we don't really sell retained recruitment that was quite an achievement, the marketing has been so successful that potential clients are calling us, we have had to put the marketing on stop as we are unable to cope with so many leads in a short period of time. If you are tired of cold calling and would like to discover how to have your clients calling you I would recommend drewcoaching."*

Steve Hauge
Foundation Resourcing

 *"I appointed Terry in October 2010 as my Business Coach and since that day I have never looked back. He has been motivating in both my business life and at home. He has helped me find the focus I needed to see through all the everyday 'firefighting' that can 'cloud' your judgement and made me realise that by taking responsibility for your actions and in-actions everyday, you will achieve your goals. 'Goals' is also another watch word with Terry, without them there is no destination and whilst anyone can set goals, Terry will enable you to exceed them in everyway. In addition to the weekly coaching sessions, he is always available to provide guidance at the end of the phone. His knowledge of marketing, his reason to be and the value of time has made a significant difference to the results I am seeing in my business. Terry you are an inspiration and a star."*

Melanie Bose
Omnium IT Recruitment Limited

"I find the marketing tips and information Terry shares interesting and really get a lot of value and benefit from them, I have often forwarded them on to others and  *just find them a good read. Not too much information and not too long and "waffling" I find that I feel like I know who you are, really enjoy your writing. I would be happy to recommend Terry to other Recruitment/Search Firms... I work closely with a number of other recruiters and search firms, I find that in this economy we need to and benefit from working together. I do a number of splits with other agencies, I think we need to change how we see and do things, I have been so grateful to be able to get help and to give help to other colleagues, I think we all need to get an "abundance" mentality...lets all work together and share... a half a loaf of bread is far better than no bread at all."*

Debra Manson
Debra Manson Recruitment & Training

"I have only been working with Terry for a few months but he has already transformed my thinking and the results are now there to see. He has a clear understanding of what needs to be done and has helped me to implement a client attraction system that works. I would happily recommend Terry to any non competitor of mine."

Lee Hancock
i4C Executive Search Limited

"22 leads in just 5 days... Without making a single cold call! – Terry delivers what he say's he's going to and that's all you can ask for..."

Kate Bailey
Cranleigh Personnel

"Terry provides a friendly voice giving me insights into the recruitment industry and ideas on marketing based on his no-nonsense, problem solving approach."

Richard Brown
Grassroots Recruitment

Contents

Introduction   **5**
   Why This Book?   5
   How to Use This Book   9

Deadly Threat # 1 Your Attitude and Beliefs   **13**
   The Power of Positive Attitude   14

**Deadly Threat # 2 Not Knowing Where Your
Business is Going**   **19**
   Why People Don't Set Goals   20
   Taking Action   31
   Key Performance Indicators   32

**Deadly Threat # 3 Not Understanding Your
Power of Influence**   **37**
   Influencing with Integrity   37
   The Six Weapons of Influence   42
   Accelerated Sales Process in Action   53

Deadly Threat # 4 Not Having a Niche   **59**
   How to Pick a Niche   60

Deadly Threat # 5 Poor Communications   **67**
   Direct Mail   71
   E-Shots   71
   Website   72
   Payper Click (PPC)   79
   Social Media (LinkedIn, Twitter & Facebook) 79
   Remarketing   83
   Joint Venture/Strategic Allegiance Host Beneficiary 83
   The Systemasized Referral Process System   85

Contents

Thought Leadership   87

Get Free Advertising Using PR   88

Deadly Threat # 6 Not Having Effective Time Management   **93**

A Time Audit   95

Make a Decision   98

Deadly Threat # 7 Not Knowing What you *Should* Know   **103**

How to Manage to The Sales Process, to Make More Placements and Create a Business of Value   105

Other Little Known Threats to YOU and The Recruitment/Search Firm Industries   114

Conclusion   **119**

Pareto Principle   120

Next steps! (Wait, there's more!)   **125**

About the Author   **126**

Acknowledgements   **127**

References   **128**

Introduction

"It is your decisions, and not your conditions, that determine your destiny."
Anthony Robbins

Why This Book?

As an owner of a Recruitment/Search Firm Business, it is imperative that you read every word of this book.

Not only that you read it, but you must take action and answer all the questions.

Please don't put this book down and think, *I will read this later.*

How many times have you done that before, only never to read the book you so wanted to at the time?

This time it could be too late, and the consequences could be dire.

A recent study has shown that you are, right now, facing SEVEN distinct and deadly threats to your business, and if you don't handle them now, then the chances are high that your business will become just another statistic and join the thousands of others on the scrapheap.

The sad fact is that 80% of Recruitment/Search Firms go bust in the first five years of trading. There's a reason for this, but I'll come to this in a moment.

That's the bad news.

The good news is you can quickly and easily avoid every single one of these deadly threats if you're both able to recognize them and take the right action when you see them.

The best news of all is they're not difficult to spot. Avoiding them doesn't cost a lot in time or money, and the cure is almost immediate.

However, if you don't get this seventh fundamental threat handled first, then you and your business won't be in a position to tackle the other six.

So that's why this book has been written for you. *The 7 Deadly Threats to Your Recruitment/Search Firm in the new economy and How to Avoid Them.*

It shows the results of research into these *7 Deadly Threats* in detail, and also shares with you some simple, fast, and effective ways of avoiding them completely so you can become a more profitable business.

The 7 deadly threats your Recruitment/Search Firm business faces, are:

1. Your attitude and beliefs

2. Not knowing where your business *is going*

3. Not understanding your Power of Influence

4. Not having a niche

5. Poor communications – better marketing

6. Not having effective time management

The Seventh Hidden Threat

The list above is slightly misleading; because there is actually a seventh hidden and fundamental threat that research shows underpins the six you see listed above.

And this **seventh** fundamental threat is <u>your own false assumptions about your business and what it takes to succeed in these difficult economic times.</u> This false assumption is that *'If you are a good recruiter you will have a successful and profitable Staffing/Recruitment Business'*

That's a BIG FAT LIE and the **number one threat** to your business!

7. Not knowing what you should know

Why most independent Recruitment/Search Businesses fail and what to do about it

(A true story- some of the names have been removed to protect those involved)

One day, 19 years ago, on a rainy spring afternoon in London, two men attended a seminar for budding Recruitment Business owners.

They were very much alike, these two men. Both wanted to make a difference in the Recruitment world, both were friendly and people-focused, and both had big dreams for their future Recruitment Businesses.

They vowed to stay in touch. But as the years rolled by they gradually lost contact, that was until recently when they ran into each other at a soccer match.

They were still very much alike. Both were happily married. Both had children. And unlike many who attended the same Recruitment Business seminar, both had started their own Recruitment Businesses AND were still in business, despite the ups and downs of the economy. Both also had excellent reputations for being great recruiters.

But there was a striking difference...

One of the men worked in his business for 40-50 hours a week and made a modest income for his family. The other spent more time with his family than he did working, and enjoyed a multimillion-pound Recruitment Business.

What made the difference?

Have you ever wondered, as I have, what makes this kind of difference in people's lives? It isn't always intelligence, or hard work, or luck. And it certainly isn't that one person wants success and the other doesn't.

***The difference lies in what each person knows, and
how they make use of that knowledge.***

The first man – who worked very hard to bring home a modest income for his family – had become an expert on the latest techniques in Recruitment, you name it, and he did it!

The second man – who had achieved all his financial goals – had become an expert on marketing.

The first man had become a master of his craft and had a job, while the second man had become a master at bringing in new clients and candidates, getting bigger deals, and had built a business that did not rely on his personal billings.

The first man took pride in doing every job himself – he had to make sure it was done right, while the second man – with his higher revenues – took pride in hiring highly skilled people to be a part of his team and to be excellent in the areas where he was weak. He also discovered the importance of systemizing his business, so he never had to recruit experienced recruiters.

The first man's business was his life; it constantly interfered with his relationships and his health. He also had the constant challenge of never being able to find good consultants, and only getting business by 'cold calling', while the second man's business enabled him to create the lifestyle he dreamed of 19 years ago.

Every month his business would generate hundreds of leads, and his consultants never ever made cold calls. In fact, pestering potential clients with cold calls was banned.

How do I know this? Because the second man in the story is **me** from many years ago!

But here's the reason why I tell you this true story...

This exact same story will be repeated in hundreds of Recruitment Firms over the next few years.

Many new Recruitment Business Owners will start and HAVE

A RECRUITMENT JOB RATHER THAN A RECRUITMENT BUSINESS... only to struggle to find the clients, struggle to make ends meet, and either stay trapped in a job they hate, not being able to make the leap to having a business rather than a job, or worse, have to go back to the job they left because they can no longer pay the bills. If they're lucky, perhaps they'll make a bit more money than they did at their former job, but will have more stress and work to go along with it.

The purpose of this book is to allow YOU to discover the secrets the most successful Recruitment and Search Firms know, and what you can do to make more placements, earn more money and create a successful business.

How to Use This Book

Before you begin, imagine that you have just arrived in your office on a sunny Monday morning. You place your freshly made coffee on the side and open up your emails. As you do so, there is a constant stream of emails from potential clients who wish to speak to you about your services. How would you feel? What would that mean to you and your family? What impact would that have on your finances? What would you be saying to yourself?

The experience of sitting at your computer, drinking your coffee and watching sales inquiries flood in is not fantasy, it's what's happening right now with your competitors! You too can have exactly the same experience, but for you to achieve that, you must make the decision to generate sales leads on a regular and consistent basis, and create a business rather than a job.

Consider this:

1% of Recruitment/Search Owners become wealthy in their lifetimes - 4% become financially independent - the other 95% accomplish neither.

That means 95% of people are generally wrong!

So if you want to be successful in your Recruitment/Search Business, simply do the opposite of what everyone else is doing. And guess what? It really works!

The tragedy of the 'Herd Mentality'

Earl Nightingale, in his famous audio program, *'The Strangest Secret'*, says the reason people fail is *conformity*.

The problem is, that everyone is trying to act like everyone else, and with 95% of people not achieving worthwhile success; conformity is a sure-fire way to fail.

Do what successful Recruitment Business Owners do, and you will have what successful Recruitment Business Owners have.

Deadly Threat # 1
Your Attitude and Beliefs

"Our deepest fear is not that we are inadequate. Our deepest fear is that we are powerful beyond measure. It is our light, not our darkness, that most frightens us. We ask ourselves, who am I to be brilliant, gorgeous, talented and fabulous? Actually, who are you not to be? Your playing small doesn't serve the world. There's nothing enlightened about shrinking so that other people won't feel insecure around you. We are all meant to shine, as children do... It's not just in some of us; it's in everyone. And as we let our own light shine, we subconsciously give other people permission to do the same. As we're liberated from our own fear, our presence automatically liberates others."

Marianne Williamson

Deadly Threat # 1
Your Attitude and Beliefs

Your success is your choice.

Research has shown that this is the number one reason why Recruitment Business Owners have so much success. Even when things are tough, and all the experts are predicting doom and gloom, the Recruitment Business Owner that asks empowering questions such as;

1. Over the next 90 days, what three things can we do to increase sales?

2. Who are the 100 top potential clients we should speak to?

3. What seven things am I grateful for right now in my life?

...is a business owner with the right attitude for success.

Attitudes drive behaviour. *Your results are the result of your mental attitude.* When you choose your attitude, you consciously (or unconsciously) send out that message and it's loud and clear for people to see.

Almost always, you have a choice as to what attitude to adopt. There is nothing in any normal work situation that dictates you must react one way or another. If you feel angry about something that happens, that's how you choose to feel. Nothing in the event itself makes it absolutely necessary for you to feel that way, it's your choice. And since you do have a choice, most of the time you'll be better off if you choose to react in a positive, rather than a negative way.

People spend a lifetime searching for happiness; looking for peace. They chase idle dreams, addictions, religions and even other people, hoping to fill the emptiness that plagues them. The irony is the only place they ever needed to search was within.

The Power of Positive Attitude

It's not what happens to you that counts; it's how you react to what happens to you, especially when you experience unexpected problems of any kind. Learn and master powerful mind strategies you can use to keep yourself thinking and acting positively and creatively.

Positive attitude means longer life

If you want to live a longer healthier life, then you need to develop and maintain a positive attitude. It's now a fact, thanks to a study from two American Universities. Researchers followed and studied 1500 people for seven years. All 1500 were in good health when the study started. They studied how they aged, by measuring such things as weight loss, walking speed, and exhaustion.

What exactly did they discover? They found that people who maintained a positive attitude were significantly less likely to show signs of aging were less likely to become frail and were more likely to be stronger and healthier than those who had a negative attitude. If you have a doom and gloom attitude you're actually killing yourself, and at the very least, your negative attitude is just making you weaker.

So if you want a successful Recruitment Business, make a decision today to be happy and successful. It's your choice.

Action Steps

Since the attitude you have is due to your decision, here are the questions to ask and answer honestly, that are guaranteed to improve your attitude. Get in touch with what is really important.

- What did your business bill/invoice over the last 12 months?

- What **do you want to bill**/invoice over the next 12 months?

- What's the difference in money between what you billed/invoiced over last 12 month and what you want to bill /invoice in next 12 months?

  (Whatever that number is multiply that by the number of years you plan to have your business. That number is what it WILL cost you if you continue to do what you're doing).

- What decision will you make in the next 24 hours that will reduce the gap between where you are now and where you want to be in 12 months from now?

- What are the actions steps you'll take to reduce the gap?

Spend some time answering these questions in *as much detail as possible.*

Deadly Threat # 2
Not Knowing Where Your
Business *is Going*

"Champions aren't made in gyms. Champions are made from something they have deep inside them, a desire, a dream, a vision. They have to have the skill and the will. But the will must be stronger than the skill."
Muhammad Ali

Deadly Threat # 2
Not Knowing Where Your Business is Going

"People with goals succeed because they know where they are going. It's as simple as that."
Earl Nightingale

The number one reason why most independent Recruitment/Search Businesses fail is…

They don't know where they're going and if you don't know where you're going how will you know when you get there?

Let me explain.

Nearly every audio program, video program, book and seminar on the subject of personal development and business success covers the idea of goal setting.

And yet, despite all the information available about this subject, I've found over the years that, most Recruitment/Search Firm business owners have not set goals for their business.

And for those who have written their goals on paper, many of them haven't kept up to date with the actions or measured them against good records as to where they are against their goals.

It's often been said that successful people set goals.

I've been very fortunate, over the years, to have interviewed many successful Recruitment Business Owners. The one thing that seems to be the common theme amongst them is that they each have a well-defined goal so they know exactly where they're going.

A story for you…

There is an alleged story from 1954. A group of students who were graduating from Harvard University were asked a series of questions. One of these questions was: *"Do you have a well-*

defined goal that's written down?"

87% said that they did NOT have goals, 10% said that they had goals but that those goals weren't written down, and only 3% said that they had WRITTEN goals.

Some 20 years later these same respondents were interviewed and asked a variety of questions about their lives. The 3%, who had written their goals down all those years before, were now worth more when put together, than the other 97%.

Now you and I know that money is only one measure of success, and that every single person can have his or her own definition of success. What was also interesting about this study was that the 3% who had well-defined goals were happier and more content than the entire 97%.

It must make you think that there really is something about goal setting that makes a major difference to our individual success and therefore, to the success of our Recruitment Businesses.

In all the years ***drewcoaching*** has been coaching Recruitment Business Owners/directors, we have never ever met a successful Recruitment Business Owner who didn't have a well-defined goal, and who didn't know exactly what the business would look; sound and feel like when it was finished.

Why People Don't Set Goals

So before we look at how to set our goals, let's look at the reasons why people don't set them, and why, if they do, some people don't keep them up to date.

Over the years I've asked thousands of Recruitment/Search Firm Owners why they don't set goals and below is a sample of the answers.

Perhaps if you haven't yet set goals, or if you have but struggled to keep up to date with them, this might help you

identify some of the reasons why!

- They don't know how to do it.
- They fear failure.
- They fear success, perhaps believing that success brings more problems, that their friends will be jealous and stop liking them.
- They're too impatient, but as you and I know success comes one step at a time.
- They think their major goals are unattainable.
- Fear of rejection.
- They don't make time to do it.
- They have self-limiting beliefs.
- They think that goal setting isn't important.
- They have no ambition.

So knowing that goal setting is important, here are some areas for you to consider setting goals for:

1. Career
2. Skill improvement
3. Time usage
4. Fitness
5. Health
6. Personal relationships
7. Leisure
8. Sports
9. Travel
10. Commercial goals

11. Financial success

12. Learning to speak in public

13. Increasing vocabulary

14. Negotiation or selling skills

15. Management skills

16. Body language

17. Creativity

Goal setting is for anything and everything you want to achieve. It's essential that your personal goals are in alignment with your commercial goals.

The most common goal setting areas are what I call the 3 F"s:

1. Fitness

2. Finance/business

3. Family

It has been found that having goals in these three areas brings balance and fulfilment to your life.

The Reticular Activation System

The marvelous thing about setting goals, having a direction, and knowing what we want, is that we engage a part of our brain called the *Reticular Activation System*

I'm sure you'll have had the following happen to you:

You've decided to buy something, and then suddenly you see that same item everywhere. Perhaps the commonest occurrence of this is when you're about to take delivery of a new car. Suddenly you see that same car everywhere, the same model, even the same color!

Why?

Simply because you've opened your mind (your reticular activation system) to that information.

Perhaps you've booked a holiday and then start to see information about that place that you've never noticed before.

Once we focus on something, then we notice more about that subject or object. That's what happens when we set goals. We start to hear and see things that will help us to achieve them. Those things were there before; we just didn't know that we needed them because we hadn't set our goals and told ourselves that we were interested in that information.

So let's look at some of the best ways to set goals:

1. <u>Goals must be written down</u>

Why?

Simply because once they're written down you can audit them. You can read them on a regular basis; you can check that you're on track to their accomplishment. If they're not written down, they're just dreams, not goals!

2. <u>When you write your goals, make certain that they're written in **positive language**, without linguistic negatives and in the **present tense**.</u>

Positive Language

If you write goals in negative language or use linguistic negatives it's extremely hard for your mind to form a picture of the outcome you want.

Can you form a picture for the word 'not', meaning not doing something? It's difficult to do. It's far better to create a picture of what you want and use the power of language to provide a clear picture.

If you have a goal to give up something, then instead of saying: *"I will not smoke,"* which can only reinforce the habit, re word it, to a reward based goal like; *"I would like to have a healthy body"* or *"my partner enjoys holding me as I smell so much better."*

Write goals in the present tense, rather than the future tense.

If you set a goal that says, *"I will be..."* or *"I will have..."*

The words – *"will be"* or *"will have"*, indicate something in the future, not something that will ever come to pass. So every time you read the goal it will always be positioned in the future. It's far better to say, *"The date is..."* and state a future date while using the terms *"I have"* or *"I am"* or *"I do."* This method sets up internal pressure to perform.

So to recap:

- ✓ Positive language
- ✓ No linguistic negatives
- ✓ Present tense

Which goals to go for?

Here is a very simple process, which you can use immediately:

- Decide on a time frame that you want to work with; that could be one year, five years, ten years, or even a lifetime – you decide.

- Then write a question at the top of a clean page which asks: *"What do I want to have, be and do in this time frame?"*

- Then brainstorm, or brain-dump every idea you have, including places you want to go, achievements, profits, as well as personal, commercial, social or anything and everything you can think of.

- 3. <u>Prioritizing your goals</u>

Now you need to prioritize that list, and the way to do it varies, depending upon the length of the list.

If the list is short, about six or seven items, then you can easily prioritize it using numbers. If the list is long, start by simply catagorizing which of the three areas each one falls into A, B or C.

   A. Goals you <u>definitely</u> want to achieve.

   B. You would <u>like</u> to achieve

   C. Well maybe one day you'll get round to them.

Write down what you want, not what is expected of you. Then take the "A" list and prioritize that with numbers.

Ok, so let's take just your top goal and look how that should be written down. Remember that a goal is only a stake in the ground. It gives you direction, and because it's your goal you can change it at any time. Be bold, there's not much fun in achieving inconsequential goals.

Here are the steps to write out your goals, write the goal down using this formula, and make sure your goals are:

- ✓ Precise
- ✓ Exciting
- ✓ Truthful
- ✓ Effective action
- ✓ Recordable/measurable
- ✓ Affirmation (letter to the future)

I'll go through each of these ideas for you now.

1. Precise - The goal must be precise otherwise it's difficult to take aim. There's little point saying we want to be rich without knowing precisely what rich means. Obviously, rich has different meanings for different people.

So ensure that your goal has all the numbers, dates and details included, so that you know precisely what you're aiming for.

2. Exciting - The goal must be exciting. Why? Because, if the goal doesn't move you in some way, you're unlikely to stay on track. However, if it does excite you, it's far more likely that you'll continue to take action until the goal is achieved. I'll give some more detail on this part further on.

3. Truthful - The goal must be truthful. By this I mean that you must really believe that you can achieve it. As you and I know, if we don't believe that we can do something, that belief is going to stop us taking action.

So, a self-question about your belief in yourself to achieve this goal will be necessary.

4. Effective Action - The goal should involve you in Effective Action.

Yes, you may well need to involve other people in helping you achieve your goal, but there must be personal commitment to action; action that will take you to your goal; not just any old action, but effective action.

Action that is clearly focused on you achieving the goal, keeping you on track, ensuring your success.

5. Recordable - The goal must be recordable, and recordable in two specific ways.

You must be able to measure or record that you have achieved the goal of course, and you must be able to *measure your progress* along the way.

Example

Imagine for a moment that you'd set a goal to go on holiday to a certain country on a certain date. You would need to know how much that trip would cost and how much, if you had to save for it, you would need to save each month or each year. That way you could measure your progress towards the goal by the monthly saving and your eventual achievement of the goal of going to the country in question.

Once you've written your goal in this way you'll know that it is precise and exciting, you believe that YOU can achieve it and that you'll need to take effective action that you can measure.

With good records you'll achieve the goal, because you'll know where you are at any time, regarding the actions and results you're achieving.

6. Affirmation/Letter to the future - The final part of the goal setting process is to write an affirmation/letter to the future.

This is simply a paragraph that affirms to yourself that you will take the actions you've decided to take, that you will achieve the goal, and that the actions and result are in alignment, with your values and beliefs.

Write a letter to your coach as if it is the date you have achieved your goal. Write your goal and letter to the future in the present tense. "I am" rather than "I will". They must include the date to be specific and they must be written in positive. Remember think about what you want. Use words like *"I love doing"* and *"I am"*.

Example

It's Sunday 10th November 2017 at 7.30am; I'm sitting at home looking at my figures for the last 11 months. We've generated £784,000k in fees for my Search and Selection business by placing senior candidates within the major accountancy firms.

The average fee is £21,000. With what's also in the pipeline this is my best year yet. I work mainly with six clients, who are also good friends. I have become more focused, determined and successful, by taking positive and consistent action every day. This goal was achieved by talking to my regular clients, seeking referrals from both clients and candidates, and resulted in acquiring three new clients over the last 12 months. I'm well rested and feel happy, secure and at peace. The next 12 months will be even better.

Actions to be taken that will take you towards your goals

A couple of years ago I took up running and really enjoyed the obvious benefits such as extra energy, managing weight and overall well-being.

After a couple of months I thought I would enter a few local races (the why) to keep the motivation going. With that in mind I went online and found details of a number of coaches.

I then called them asking them a series of questions. When it came to what they offered, the price was pretty much the same and the service was pretty similar. I eventually went with a trainer called Steve. The main reason for this was he indicated that he had a coach himself to keep him on check with his goals.

A business coach can be your secret weapon in expanding your business or making your career flourish, whether you need advice on website design, creating marketing strategies, or help in learning the skills to set effective goals. Consider hiring a business coach as a positive step towards reaching your full business potential. As a behind-the-scenes advisor, your business coach can help you earn more money, operate your business more smoothly, or become a more effective leader.

If you would like some **FREE** online coaching simply go to www.drewcoaching.com/sevendeadlythreats/ and register for your two week email coaching program.

But here is the main reason why it pays to invest in a coach, (and most successful Recruitment/Search Firm Business Owners have a coach or a mentor) as the boss you may well say this is what I'm going to do by the end of the day, but who is there to hold you accountable if you don't? With a mentor or coach at your side, it's much harder to let this happen as you've got someone metaphorically looking over your shoulder, holding you accountable for your daily actions!

Yesterday's Road

Some years ago a client I was working with came up with the *Yesterday's Road Method*. Let me share it with you now.

I believe that you and I know ourselves better than anyone else, that we already know the majority of actions we need to take to achieve our goals, and that all we need to do is to ask ourselves the right questions to easily establish the precise actions to take.

It's simple to do and yet incredibly effective.

This is how it was originally used.

My client had sold a business and was in the process of the earn-out year.

Half way through the year she lost a major client and it looked for a while as though she wouldn't hit the projected figures. This would have cost her, the other directors and shareholders a great deal of money.

We called the director team together and said this:

"Imagine that it's now the end of the year and we haven't hit the figures, we aren't going to get the second chance to earn our money"

So, I want you to answer this question:

"If only I'd ... we would have reached our target"

What are those dots?

Now you'll notice that the expression is: *"If only I'd"* not, *"If only we"* or *"If only they"* or *"If only the government"* or *"If only the weather"*. **It's about taking personal responsibility for our actions and results.**

In half an hour, the directors had completed their reports in answer to that question, and we then put all the answers together, developed a plan for each day of the remaining six months, and by taking the actions that everyone knew they should take, we soared through the figures.

It's that simple.

So to establish the actions you need to take to achieve your goal, briefly imagine that you're at the point where you should have achieved the goal and you haven't, then ask yourself that powerful question:

"If only I'd... I would have achieved this goal."

Then write down anything that comes to mind. Within those notes will be the actions you know you need to take.

This idea helps to establish the actions to achieve anything. When working with a team to work out what could be done, then it's just brilliant, and so effective to have a number of people working on the same idea.

I know once you've tried this method you too will use it many times to know what actions to take.

Taking Action

*"It's not knowing what to do,
it's doing what you know."*
Tony Robbins

So you've set your well-defined goals and you know exactly what your business will look like in one to five years from now.

If you believe that's it, I have some news for you. Setting the goal is only the first step. Now you must take ACTION. Once you know where your business is going, you can now look at, and decide on the action steps that you'll need to take to achieve your goals. Deciding what you're going to do and when, will bring results.

A 'To-Do' list

A written 'to-do' list is a simple technique that can increase your productivity by 20% or more, if you don't use it already. It also has extra benefits of clearing your mind and saving you energy and stress.

Spend 15-20 minutes each day on planning your activities with a daily to-do list. Start your day with it. Even better, every evening write a plan for the next day, listing your daily tasks. It is important that you actually write down your tasks. Some people are more comfortable doing it on paper, while others prefer using a computer. Try and see what works best for you.

After you've listed all your tasks, review your to-do list and decide on the priority of each task. Give higher priority to the tasks that get you closer to your goals.

A proven simple technique is an ABC rating of your priorities. Mark the tasks on your to-do list with 'A's' if they're critical for your goals and simply must be done that day (or else you face serious consequences). 'B's' are less urgent, but still important tasks that you should start right after you're finished with 'A's'. 'C's' are 'nice to do' things that you could do if you have any time left after 'A's' and 'B's.' Those tasks can be safely moved to another day.

Here's one important tip to keep in mind, if during the day some new unplanned task comes up, don't do anything until you put that new task on your list and rate it by priority. See it written amongst the other tasks and put it in perspective. The more you let go of the urge to skip that simple step, the more productive and satisfied you become.

<u>When making a to-do list, break down your complex tasks into smaller manageable pieces, and focus on one task at a time.</u> Finally, after completion of a task take a moment to look at the results and feel the satisfaction of the progress.

Actions that will take me closer to achieving my goals:

Take a piece of blank paper (or do this on the computer if you prefer) and create a table, three columns wide, by ten (or however many rows you need) Then head column one; Action. Column two; Outcome and by when, and then the third column, Comments.

Here's what it could look like:

Action	Outcome by when	Comments

Key Performance Indicators

KPIs (Key Performance Indicators) are the key factors that indicate the health of the business and its ability to meet its objectives. Originally developed in the 1960's by a team at McKinsey, the concept of KPIs was to identify and monitor the factors most critical to the success of the business, and therefore giving the business the ability to build and sustain a competitive advantage.

By understanding what the key factors for success are, they can then be measured. KPI's are therefore a set of metrics that a business can use to assess its likelihood of meeting its mission.

Below are the typical activities that are measured by successful Recruitment Firm;

- Client Calls
- Candidate Calls
- CV's Sent
- Client Visits
- Client Interviews
- Candidate Interviews
- Vacancies working on
- Revenue

Within the industry there is a lot of resistance to KPI's. Recruiters argue that they would much rather work in a non KPI-driven environment, as they don't need policing and know what needs to be done. However, as the owner of the business, you should be looking to create a business that's scalable, with predictable income that has some real value should you decide to sell.

Besides which, we all know what needs to be done; however we often don't do what we know we should do. So it is imperative you have well-defined KPI's.

It has been shown that this will not only increase the productivity of your business, but it also means that you'll be less reliant on having to recruit experienced recruiters, as you can now bring in individuals with the right attitude. Once your business is systematized with well-defined KPI's that are adhered to, you have a high value scalable business with a predictable income.

If you can't measure it you can't manage it.

Action Steps

As a Recruitment/Search Firm Business Owner, you know exactly what needs to be done to ensure your objectives are achieved.

Below are some examples of some KPI's that you can implement into your business.

Your action steps for this section are, try to implement some of the examples below into your business, as well as getting into the habit of writing a 'to do' list everyday, to keep track of your productivity. Then look at how you can increase that productivity over time.

- How many client calls does a consultant need to do a day to achieve their goal?

- How many candidate calls does a consultant need to do to achieve their goal?

- How many CV's should a consultant send for each job order?

- How many client visits?

- How many client interviews?

- How many candidate interviews?

- Vacancies/job orders working on?

- What is the weekly revenue target?

- What do you believe a consultant should be doing so that once they do it they will achieve their goal?

Deadly Threat # 3
Not Understanding Your
Power of Influence

"Seek first to understand then to be understood."
Stephen Covey

Deadly Threat # 3
Not Understanding Your Power of Influence

"Influencing with integrity is winning the hearts and minds of others so they want exactly the same thing as you."
Terry Edwards

Influencing with Integrity

Have you ever wondered why another Search/Recruitment Firm in exactly the same sector as you is growing year on year? Your firm constantly comes up against them, in fact, they're probably your number one competitor, and it feels as if they have the edge as they always seem to get the business you're after.

There is a very good reason why that's happening and I'm going to share the secrets with you. When you read this section and commit to mastering the skills required, you'll make more placements, earn more money and work fewer hours.

Did you notice the caveat?

It's all very well reading this and thinking that's great, now I now know what needs to be done to enjoy more success. However, if you do **nothing** with the information and keep doing what you have always done, *you'll have what you always have had.*

If you want to inspire others in your team, or if you simply want to discover how to influence with integrity and have fantastic relationships with friends, colleagues and clients read on.

The ability to influence is one of the most highly sought after skills, be it in business, to influence your clients or team, or perhaps at home with your partner and children. Studies have shown that individuals who are able to master the skill of influencing with integrity, are able to move up the corporate ladder quicker, have better relationships and generally seem to be happier. The ability to influence means that you get more clients, earn more money and have better relationships.

With the ability to influence, you're able to let others know what it is you want to accomplish. You have the ability to motivate and inspire others as well as resolve conflict.

Over the years, we have had the opportunity to work with some of the top performing Recruitment/Search Business Firms in the world. *Drewcoaching* have modelled the techniques that work and we share them with you. We will also share with you techniques that have been discovered by social psychologists.

Over the years, we have all seen and heard masters in the art of influencing with integrity. I sometimes wonder what type of world we would live in without masters such as Nelson Mandela, Bill Gates, Margaret Thatcher, Ghandi, Winston Churchill and Martin Luther King.

Let me ask you, what type of life would you have if you mastered these techniques and could always influence with integrity?

Here are 7 tips to help you get started:

Tip #1. Remember the name of the person you get introduced to

Imagine the scene; you've just been introduced to one of the Directors of your largest client at a corporate event. As the day progresses you get an opportunity to share a drink with them. However, although you were introduced less than two hours before, you've forgotten their name! Tell me, do you think that matters? Of course it does. Just imagine that if every time you met someone you could commit their name to your memory forever.

Well you can by using these simple and effective techniques:

1. *Commit* – to remembering every person's name, make that decision now! If you have always told yourself you're lousy at remembering names – it's true. If you now tell yourself that you always remember names – it's true. Whatever you believe is true to you.

2. *Concentrate* – pay attention to the name that you're told. If you didn't hear it, ask them to repeat it. If you find the name unusual ask them to spell it to you. Better still, have a note pad with you and write the name down as it is spelt to you. As you're given the person's name get a clear and detailed picture of that person. Then imagine their name is written across their forehead. Note the person's physical characteristics. Use all your senses to form a lasting impression.

3. *Repeat* – Repetition helps engrave the name in your memory.

- Use the name silently to yourself
- Make a comment on the name if possible
- Use the name in conversation
- Use it when leaving

How successful would you be if you mastered this skill so well that it became second nature?

Tip #2. *"Seek first to understand then to be understood."* *Stephen Covey*

When communicating, spend your time understanding what that person is saying and what they want. We all understand that in an ideal world our decisions are based on logic and sound reasoning. In the real world, people act in response to their personal preferences, feelings and social influences, and sometimes they're not even aware of it.

Find common ground. Listening is crucial to influencing with integrity, by demonstrating that your values, aspirations and concerns are the same as theirs. This shows that you can see things from their point of view and have empathy.

Tip # 3. Show you really care for the person that you want to influence.

This applies if you're at home or at work. When you show that you really care for the person that you're influencing, they're more likely to accept another point of view. Interestingly, when they believe you care about them, they're more likely to offer you more information, thus enabling you to influence them.

Tip # 4. How to never lose another argument

This technique is quite simple and has a 100% success rate.

DO NOT ARGUE WITH ANYONE AT ANY TIME!

It really is that simple. You may well win the argument, but that's all you're going to win. If you decide that you don't have to be right, you'll never argue again and that way you'll never lose an argument.

Tip #5. *"Begin with the end in mind."* Stephen Covey

Begin with the end in mind when you start the conversation, negotiation or influencing. As simple as it sounds, it really is extremely effective. By knowing your desired outcome you can take the appropriate steps to get there. The most successful influencers do this every time.

Seek the win/win on every occasion. If you win and the client wins that's great. If either party believe that they have lost in some way, you're simply storing problems for later. By doing your research and understanding what is negotiable, you can offer something that's valuable.

Tip #6. There is a stereotypical image of a sales person

Often the term that's used is 'gift of the gab'. Whilst undoubtedly the ability to communicate effectively with clients and potential clients is important, what's even more important is to understand what the needs of the clients are.

Let me explain in more detail. **All human beings are motivated to avoid pain and gain pleasure.**

A client of mine who is a Recruitment consultant complained that whenever she visited clients they would sit on the fence about deciding who to use. I explained that what she needed to do was establish what the client's pain was regarding recruitment.

The real skill is influencing in such a way so that your client wants to buy more from you than you want to sell to them.

Time and time again, business people have been taught about features, benefits and USP's (unique selling propositions). Whilst these do have a part in influencing your clients, the real skill is having the client wanting to buy from you more than you want to sell to them.

Please pay extra attention

It is easier to sell the avoidance of pain than it is to sell the gaining of pleasure.

You see *"away motivation is the catalyst for action, towards motivation is the continuation of action."*

Psychologists have found this to be the most effective method for getting your clients to want to buy from you more than you want to sell.

Tip #7. Rapport

I'm sure you have been in a situation where you've met someone for the first time and afterwards you felt that you didn't like them or they weren't your kind of person. If I were to ask you why, usually you would have trouble explaining why that was. Equally, I'm sure you've met someone and within minutes you felt completely at ease with them.

I can assure you this is not coincidence. When you get on with someone you are in rapport with them. This creates a climate of trust and understanding which is vital for influencing. Psychologists have discovered precisely what needs to happen for you to be in rapport with someone, enabling you to trust and understand them and vice-versa.

Rapport is a form of influence. When you're communicating with someone, once you're in rapport, they will do all that they can to see your point of view. The quality of the rapport you have will influence the quality of influence. Interestingly, most of what's going on when you're in rapport with someone is happening unconsciously.

The Six Weapons of Influence

"Here's where the emotional triggers come in."
Robert Cialdini

Researcher and author Robert Cialdini, describes the *Six Weapons of Influence*, (in his book, *Influence: Science and Practice)* as reciprocation, commitment and consistency, social proof, liking, authority and scarcity. As these are such powerful 'weapons' I'm now going to share with you my take on these six influences.

1. RECIPROCATION - *"The Old Give and Take-and Take"*

All of us are taught that we should find some way to repay others for what they do for us. Most people will make an effort to avoid being considered a moocher, ingrate, or person who does not pay their debts.

This is an extremely powerful tactic and can even spur unequal exchanges. In one experiment, for example, half the people attending an art appreciation session were offered a soft drink. Afterwards, all were asked if they would buy 25-cent raffle tickets. Guess what? The people who had been offered the soft drinks purchased twice as many raffle tickets, whether or not they had accepted the drinks!

You probably already use this principle, but it's much stronger than you suspect. You can build a sense of indebtedness in someone by delivering a number of uninvited 'first favours' over time. They don't have to be tangible gifts. In today's world, useful information is one of the most valuable favours you can deliver.

One of the ethical ways in which you and I can use the power of reciprocation and obligation, is by providing free reports that help our potential client overcome a particular challenge. This is a brilliant way to expose our customers to our services and let them see for themselves how they can benefit. It also, as you will gather, includes the power of reciprocation.

Example:

One supermarket used this idea, with a slight twist, when selling cheese. Rather than just offering samples, it allowed customers to cut their own piece of cheese, this created far greater sales than they had ever experienced before.

What are the other ways in which you can provide free samples for your customers?

Unfortunately, or perhaps fortunately, dependent upon the business in which you're involved, uninvited gifts work just as well. I'm certain you've received direct mail that includes free pens, coins or even Christmas cards, all designed to utilize the power of obligation and reciprocation.

Now there's a very important point here - *the repayment of the obligation doesn't always equal the first favour.* Someone may provide a very small favour for you and you may repay it with value far exceeding that first favour.

In negotiations where a particular price or offer has been made and rejected, provided the seller immediately reduces the demand, this will also create obligation and reciprocation.

So how you can use this?

Well that's one of the facets behind the principle of permission marketing, where you offer your potential client a free report such as '*7 Things you must do before you engage a Search Firm.*'

If you want to get to see someone, send them a gift first.

- ✓ You could use gifts in direct mail
- ✓ You could start a meeting with a gift
- ✓ You could use the power and integrity of free samples

After all, what better way to let your customer actually experience dealing with you and your products. Make certain that you're using these ideas with integrity and also make certain that you measure the results of everything you do.

2. COMMITMENT AND CONSISTENCY - *"Hobgoblins of the Mind."*

We all have the desire to be consistent and appear as consistent human beings, this can work for and against us. We take actions that are consistent with previous actions and — importantly — we take action based on previously expressed beliefs.

Everyone uses shortcut decision-making processes in so many different areas of their lives.

Example: Let me share with you some fascinating information from Cialdini's book:

Some researchers in America went to people's houses and asked them to agree to put a large billboard in their front gardens regarding road safety. The billboard was ugly and badly designed.

As you might expect 83% refused and only 17% agreed (though from the way in which Cialdini describes the billboard I'm surprised that even 17% agreed).

So the researchers tested a different strategy.

They went to another set of houses and asked the owners if they would be prepared to put a three-inch square sign in their front windows, which said, 'Be a safe driver!' As you can imagine, most said, *"Yes."*

Then, a couple of weeks later, the researchers went back and asked the people who had previously agreed to the three-inch sign, if they would be prepared to have the ugly billboard in their front gardens and amazingly, or perhaps not so, 76% agreed.

Not only is this fascinating information, the fact that 76% said yes, but you and I can use this idea with integrity, to increase sales conversion rates, and thereby *increase turnover and profits.*

Once people have made a choice or taken a stand, they're under both internal and external pressure to behave consistently with that commitment. This desire for consistency offers us all a shortcut to action as we recall a previous decision we have already made.

When you can get someone to commit verbally to an action, the chances go up sharply that they'll actually do it. For example, before starting your next meeting, ask each person to commit to following the posted agenda. Then, if anyone goes off on a tangent, just ask them to explain how it fits the agenda. If they can't, they'll quickly fall back in line.

When we are asked to take further actions, that are totally in alignment, with those previously expressed beliefs, we will use shortcut decision- making processes and take congruent action.

So how do you and I use this knowledge?

Well, during the gathering stage of your business development meeting, you need to find out the beliefs and values of your customers, regarding the product or service you're selling. Then, provided that we are asking our customers to take action or actions that are in alignment with those beliefs and values, they're far more likely to say, *"Yes!"*

Example: Selling your Recruitment Service

What questions can you ask that will have the customer telling you who they are?

"Do you use a Recruitment Firm?"

The 'yes' — indicates that the customer already believes in the concept. The next question could be: *"Why?"* A simple 'Why?' would probably be too blunt, but the answer to this 'why' type question would have the customer telling you their beliefs and values about why they use a recruitment firm, then you can capitalize on that statement about who they are.

Example questions;

➲ *"What is it about your current Recruitment Service provider you would like to see more of?"*

➲ *"What is it you would like to see less of?"*

➲ *"If I could help you overcome the number one challenge..."?*

I'm certain that you have the idea.

This is one of the most powerful ideas I can share with you. I urge you to take this thought, work with it and create a series of questions that will enable you to find out the *beliefs and values of your potential customers so you can correctly align any actions you wish the customer to take with their stated position.*

It's far easier for a customer to make a series of small decisions, rather than one BIG decision at the end of the sales conversation. Each question confirms their beliefs and values, both generally and specifically to the ideas you're putting forward.

3. SOCIAL PROOF - *"Truths Are Us"*

We decide what is correct by noticing what other people think is correct. This principle applies especially to the way we determine what constitutes the correct behaviour. If everyone else is behaving in a certain way, we assume that's the right thing to do. For example, one of the important, and largely unconscious ways we decide what's acceptable behaviour on our current job, is by watching the people around us, especially the higher-ups or old-timers.

This principle of influence kicks in even more strongly when the situation is uncertain or people aren't sure what to do. When you can show them what others like them believe or are doing, people are more likely to take the same action. The mass suicides among the Heavens Gate followers in Southern California and the people in Jonestown are horrible examples of the negative power of this principle.

On the positive side, product endorsements are the most obvious application of social proof. If you want someone to do something for you, be sure to let them see that many other people are already doing it, or are willing to do it. Show them that others like them (and the more like them the better) believe in your product or are using it.

Let me give you some examples of how social proof prompts people to take action, and then suggest how you can use it in your various sales and business activities.

To start with, I'm sure that you've seen, as I have, the growth of testimonials in direct mail and on websites, often accompanied by a photograph of the person giving the testimonial, together with their comment, full name and even their address or contact numbers (just having the first name could make your readers question the credibility).

That's social proof; an endorsement by others that the product or service on offer has been tried by other people and works so well for them that they're prepared to state that fact publicly, and even be photographed with the product and their positive comment about it.

Often, when we start working with clients, there is some reluctance to do this for fear of telling their competitors who they're working with, but when you realize that when a client gives you a testimonial, it helps cement the relationship, and the client is unlikely to go elsewhere, does it matter?.

Lastly, try and get as many testimonials as possible, as those in the audience who are being exposed to the opportunity for the first time will hopefully be able to identify with at least one person who has given a testimonial. And will therefore be saying to themselves, *"If they can do it and they're like me... then I can probably do it too!"*

This is the power of social proof.

Please go to www.drewcoaching.com/sevendeadlythreats/ to get the six questions you **MUST** ask to get powerful and compelling social proof.

4. LIKING - *"The Friendly Thief"*

People love to say 'yes' to requests from people they know and like. And people tend to like others who appear to have similar opinions, personality traits, background, or lifestyle. More people will say 'yes' to you if they like you, and the more similar to them you appear to be, the more likely they are to like you.

Cialdini discovered 4 Key Factors in the Liking Principle.

The 4 Key Factors in the liking principle:

1. Physical attractiveness

2. Similarity

3. Compliments

4. Familiarity

Physical Attractiveness

When people are attractive we credit them with other positive characteristics — this is called the 'Halo Effect'. Because they're attractive we also tend to believe that they're honest, that they have high integrity and that what they say is believable.

So whilst attractiveness is in the eye of the beholder, it is up to you and I to do our best to look our best at all times. One piece of research even indicated that juries gave lighter fines to attractive defendants. Is it any wonder then that defendants are coached by their lawyers, and dressed to impress?

Similarity

This is similarity in:

- Opinions
- Dress
- Background
- Lifestyle
- Recreational activities

Basically everything!

What can you find out about potential business partners or customers that you have in common? This builds rapport or Liking!

One simple way to create similarity is in dress. If a potential customer is in shirtsleeves, then it would make sense for you to remove your jacket.

Compliments

When people pay us compliments we like them, it's that simple!

Most people are also phenomenal suckers for flattery, even when they know it isn't true. When we have a good opinion of ourselves, we can accept praise and like those who provide it. Those with low self-esteem reject even well-earned praise and distrust the source. All salespeople worth their salt have mastered the flattery tactic. They know it works, but they may not know why.

However, here's a thought for you; when paying compliments, don't compliment the person, compliment the action. Compliments of the person sound like flattery; compliments of the action and result sound far more sincere, which of course they should be.

Familiarity

We tend to say, "yes" more easily to people with whom we have regular contact, in a positive environment, which is why social days with clients can work so well. Days at sporting events, days at the races, going to the theatre, almost anything.

People also tend to like and trust anything familiar. The best way to build this familiarity is to have frequent, pleasant contacts. For example, if you spend three hours straight with someone you've never met before, you would get a sense of who they are. But if you divided the same time into 30-minute segments of pleasant interaction over six consecutive weeks, you would each have a much stronger and positive knowledge about the other. You have established a comfort level, familiarity, and a history with them. Their repeated pleasant contacts with your organization's services or products helps builds familiarity and liking.

5. AUTHORITY - *"Directed Deference"*

Most of us are raised with a respect for authority, both real and implied. Sometimes, people confuse the symbols of authority (titles, appearance, possessions) with the true substance.

Some people are more strongly influenced by authority than others, and compliance can vary according to the situation. For example, it's 11:00 p.m., and the doorbell rings. Two men in police uniforms want to come in and ask you some questions. Most people respect such authority enough that they would comply, even though the Constitution says they don't have to. But if it was 3:00 a.m. and the men were in street clothes, claiming to be detectives, most of us would hesitate. The men would have to overcome our resistance with more proof of their authority, like badges or a search warrant.

You can put this general principle to use by citing authoritative sources to support your ideas. Look and act like an authority yourself. Be sure others know that your education and experience supports your ideas. Dress like the people who are already in the positions of authority that you seek.

There are three main factors of authority:

1. Titles
2. Clothes
3. Trappings

Titles

➲ Doctor

➲ Professor

➲ Director

➲ Manager

One man even reported in Cialdini's book that he didn't use his title of professor with new people, as the conversations were too dull, and they treated him with too much respect.

Can you use an appropriate title?

Clothes

One study showed that 3% more people followed a researcher onto a busy road when wearing a suit compared to when he was dressed casually.

It's essential in business and selling to wear the appropriate clothes, ones that state your authority.

Trappings

These include your desk, your car, your briefcase.

All of these state your authority. Authority figures are believed and when they're believed, people take action and compliance rates rise.

So be careful when dealing with those who appear to have authority — is the authority figure really an expert? Use these ideas with integrity when selling and having business meetings.

6. SCARCITY - *"The Rule of the Few"*

Nearly everyone is vulnerable to some form of the principle of scarcity. Opportunities seem more valuable when they're less available. Hard-to-get things are perceived as better than easy-to-get things.

For example, the object you've almost decided to buy is out of stock. The salesperson offers to check their other stores. And guess what? A store across town has one left! Do you buy it? Of course!

Whenever appropriate, you can use the Scarcity Principle. Refer to limited resources and time limits to increase the perceived value of the benefits of helping or working with you. The possibility of losing something is a more powerful motivator than of gaining something. Let others (a customer, your boss, a lover) know what they will be losing if they don't say 'yes' to your offer.

Now here's a strange fact:

If people manage to obtain the item that's scarce, they will also believe that it's better than they would have believed if, the item had been in plentiful supply.

The scarcity principle even works with information. When someone believes they know a secret they will...

1. Believe it

2. Believe it more than normal

3. Take action

How can you use the scarcity principle in your business?

The Six Weapons of Influence are incredibly powerful and can be combined in many ways. Use them whenever you approach people you want to influence (and be sure to read Professor Cialdini's book, Influence: Science, and Practice. you'll find it most entertaining as well enlightening).

Accelerated Sales Process in Action

I'm going to share some fascinating information with you that will enable you to increase sales and profits, by being more easily able to persuade other people to your point of view by expanding on the *Six Weapons of Influence* we've just looked at.

Also, you're going to discover how to overcome the most **common objections** as to why the prospect will not work with you.

You'll also discover the 19 words that, when used before any business development meeting, will improve conversion by up to 25%.

Some of these ideas are taken from the book already mentioned *(Influence: Science and Practice by Dr. Robert Cialdini)*. They're also taken from my own experiences of selling over many years, as well as those of other successful Recruitment Business Owners.

The 3 basic ideas of influence:

1. Fixed Action Patterns

2. Triggers

3. Perceptual Contrast

Fixed Action Patterns

All human beings have a habitual way of responding to certain stimuli; let me give you some examples.

Fixed action example:

If someone puts out their right hand towards you, then you'll automatically respond by grasping their hand and shaking it. Your action has been automatically triggered by their action. If someone smiles at you, usually, though not always, you'll smile back.

So you can see from just this example, that as human beings we respond automatically to certain actions taken by others. This simple concept is extremely powerful in the art and science of persuasion.

This is why body language is so important in communication, because certain body language gestures will automatically trigger certain actions by other people.

As human beings, we are finely tuned receiving devices and will respond to particular words that people use along with the tonality of those words.

I'm certain that in your private life you've asked your partner or someone close to you:

"How are you?" And their response was, *"Yeah - I'm OK!"* You'll immediately know, by the tonality that they're not OK, and no doubt your facial expression changed into a questioning one and you responded with, *"Are you sure?"* It was an automatic response on your part.

Triggers

Now let's talk about other triggers: *Price Perception.* Cialdini gives an example where a jewellery store owner left a message for one of their staff to halve the price of some jewellery that simply wasn't moving. The member of staff misread the note and doubled the price. The jewellery was sold almost immediately.

Sometimes we are triggered to take action by the higher price of an item, rather than the lower price of an item.

We have a higher perception of value based on the higher price. This is because of shortcut decision-making, everyone uses it. As things become more complicated, we use more shortcut decisions.

Just think of the majority of the decisions you make in your life? They will mostly be based on previous experiences. They will be shortcuts. What triggers or shortcuts do you use, and would it be worth re-examining some of those decisions in the light of this information?

On the commercial front, this is one of the reasons that buyers continue to buy from the same source. Having once made a calculated decision, the original decision, they continue to use a shortcut decision-making process, because it's easier than having to rethink the whole deal.

Now that you have that information, how will you communicate to make your client want to use you?

The Perception of Contrast

I'll give you a classic example of how contrast works both for us and against us:

Imagine this situation... You have three buckets of water: The one on the left contains hot water. The one on the right contains cold water. And the one in the middle contains tepid water. You put your left hand in the left-hand bucket, the hot water. You put your right hand in the right-hand bucket, the cold water and then, after a few minutes when your hands have become accustomed to the different temperatures, you plunge both hands into the middle bucket (you'll recall that the middle bucket contains tepid water).

Now a strange thing happens - your left hand, which has been in the hot water, thinks the water in the middle bucket is cold; whereas your right hand, which has been in the cold water, thinks the water in the middle bucket is hot!

That's what's called the *perception of contrast.* So how do you and I use this in business?

Well, the first thing to note is, that it's always a good idea, when selling or negotiating, to mention the highest-priced item first. Then, any subsequently-mentioned items would seem lower by contrast.

For example, if you're selling a retained/non-retained, the more expensive retained should be sold first, as that's what the client will focus on, thus making the non-retained search more attractive.

Action Steps

1. Make getting into rapport with your clients and candidates the priority.

2. Create something of high perceive value for the client and candidate, that you can give away. Some Recruitment Firms will offer books available on Amazon in a letter/email. This gain creates that feeling of indebtedness to the client/candidate.

3. During Business development meetings ask the client questions such as:

   "What do you like most about current Recruitment Firm?"

   "What would you like them to do less of?"

   "If I could help you...?"

   These types of questions elicit commitment and consistency.

Go to www.drewcoaching.com/sevendeadlythreats and access the **Six Killer Questions** to create compelling and powerful testimonials that have clients wanting to buy from you, more than you want to sell to them.

Deadly Threat # 4
Not Having a Niche

"Originality is the by-product of sincerity."
Marianne Moore

Deadly Threat # 4
Not Having a Niche

*The narrower YOUR Recruitment niche, the broader
your recruitment business profits.*

In all my the years of experience working with some of the most successful Recruitment/Search firms, one thing I've noticed is there are some business owners that have defined their niche market, and have a clear picture of who it is they're marketing to, and there are others that tend to waiver or be unsure.

Often business owners view a niche market as narrowing their sales or cutting into a profit margin, so they fear it.

Some business owners say *"We can recruit for anyone and for any position, yep, regardless of the skill sets and experience required we can do it, after all Recruitment is Recruitment isn't it?"*

The truth is, having a well-defined niche market could be defined as a component that gives your Recruitment/Search firm Business power. A niche market allows you to define who you're marketing to.

When you know who you're marketing to, it's easy to determine where your marketing energy and dollars should be spent. Quite frankly, unless you have the marketing budget of, say, Coca Cola or Ford motoring company, you simply cannot afford to market to everyone.

You see, once you have a well-defined niche, it is also easier to market to that niche because your communication will be specific to their needs and not general, like when you're communicating to the whole business community.

How to Pick a Niche

There is an easy way to do this. Go with your passions, hobbies, interests or relevant experience. What you need to understand is what the client is looking for, and what their pain is when recruiting in this sector?

If you understand what this type of business is going to look for in your Recruitment Services, and you understand what their biggest pain is when recruiting, you'll know where to go to look for them, to find them, and to turn them into clients.

This immediately highlights your Recruitment Business as a specialist, and sets you apart from all other Recruitment Businesses, making it easier for you to market to them. Something we will cover in more detail a bit later.

Defining your niche market before you embark on your Recruitment Business is important for the following five reasons.

1. You have the ability to maximize your marketing budget by targeting your defined niche market.

2. You'll know exactly which job boards to use. You'll know where to look to find the hiring managers that are looking for your expertise, and as you can imagine this gives you a starting point.

3. Your website can then be optimized for search engines so that your niche clients and candidates can easily find you.

4. You're able to cater your website to your niche market. You can develop your site to guide your viewers and help them find solutions that you offer that are specific to the problems that your niche market is encountering right now.

5. A defined niche market makes it easier to develop ideas for new Recruitment Services that inherently

appeal to your specific niche market.

Do you now see the importance of having a niche market?

If you're still struggling with who your niche market is, then spend some time asking yourself the following questions:

> ➤ What is it that my current clients have in common?
>
> ➤ How do I set myself apart from the competition?
>
> ➤ What is different about the services that I offer?
>
> ➤ What are the 'extras' that I bring to the market?

The best way to answer these questions is not to analyze them too much.

Just write down whatever first comes to mind. Once you've completed that, then analyze the answer and it will be easy to define your niche market.

Why should your clients buy from you?

One of the many questions I ask a Recruitment Business Owner is *"What's your USP?"* and *"What can you offer your client that will give them peace of mind?"*

More often than not, the owner/director of the Recruitment Firm thinks that the USP is some kind of skin disease, or they will explain that because they're independent, they're more flexible, care about the client or the candidate... blah, blah, blah.

How having a Unique Selling Proposition (USP) will increase your sales

The Unique Selling Proposition (USP) is the number one thing that needs to be created before continuing with any other marketing endeavor. The USP is a statement or message that explains to your customers, one at a time, why they should buy from you.

The following is a list of reasons *why you must have a USP* in order to make your business prosper. One of our clients reported a 19% improvement in conversion once their USP was implemented and communicated to potential clients.

Reasons why:

- 95% of Recruitment Business Owners do not understand what a USP is, or do not have an adequate USP. Therefore, if you DO have a successful USP, then you're ahead of 95% of all your competitors.

- Your competition may be reading this right now. If you do nothing about your USP, and your competitor does, guess who wins the most sales?

- The days of the all-inclusive business are gone. There is so much choice for consumers these days, you have to show them why they should buy from you, before they walk across the street and buy from the business that does clearly state what they do!

- If there are 2 Recruitment Businesses (or worse 3-5) that offer exactly the same thing in one geographical area, and the customer cannot distinguish between the 2, 1 of them is redundant and will eventually fold. Just look around you and see the Recruitment companies that come and go because they have failed to tell the customer why they should buy from them.

- You do not want to compete on price. Some Recruitment Businesses get into the price war model where they all offer a commodity, and the only thing they have to compete with is price. Over time, you cannot sustain a business that competes on price alone. Someone will always come by and do it cheaper. If you craft your USP correctly, you can charge more than your competitors and still gain customers.

- If you're happy with your sales growth and do not want to add a single customer to your list, then continue doing what you're doing. If you're looking to outsmart the competition, possibly triple your sales in a small amount of time and not have to add a penny to your marketing efforts, then the USP is the way to go.

For some recruiters if you're new or not sure of your niche this can be challenging.

To help you create a well-defined niche market and discover if it's a good market to focus on, simply go to: www.drewcoaching.com/sevendeadlythreats/ and get the *'Search Firm & Recruiters Niching Tool'*

Action Steps

Sit down with team and answer these questions:

- Why would clients buy from us?
- What makes us stand out?
- What's our USP (having price as a USP is NOT a good idea, so don't do it)?
- How do we effectively communicate this message to our market?

Once you've done these action steps, make sure your USP is then clearly seen by your potential customers (on your website, in your literature) – as this will make you stand out from all of your competitors.

Deadly Threat # 5
Poor Communications

"The biggest problem with mass-market advertising is that it fights for people's attention by interrupting them. A 30-second spot interrupts a "Seinfeld" episode. A telemarketing call interrupts a family dinner. A print ad interrupts this article. The interruption model is extremely effective when there's not an overflow of interruptions, but there's too much going on in our lives for us to enjoy being interrupted anymore."

Seth Godin

Deadly Threat # 5
Poor Communications

"Marketing and sales isn't about trying to persuade, coerce, or manipulate people into buying your services. It is about putting yourself out in front of, and offering your services to those whom are meant to serve-people who already need and are looking for your service."
Michael Port

As a Recruitment Business Owner, if you do what other successful Recruitment Business Owners do to attract clients, to make more increased sales and earn more money, then you'll get pretty much the same outcome as other successful businesses. And you can do this without making those dreaded 'cold calls'.

As a Recruitment Business Owner, getting the most out of your marketing is vital, every marketing strategy you implement into your business needs to generate high quality leads that you can convert into more sales.

We will be sharing with you the essential marketing rules that you need to implement into every area of your marketing, in order to see the best results. We will be revealing the most cost effective and leveraged marketing strategies used by the world's most successful small business owners, that guarantee to generate you highly qualified leads and help grow your small business.

And you'll never call a cold prospect again!

Cold calling for recruiters just doesn't work as well as it used to, in part because there's so much of it, in part because your potential clients have learned to ignore it, and in part because no one likes getting a cold call from a recruiter. Also there are few recruiters who actually enjoy making cold calls.

This type of marketing is called interruption marketing where you interrupt your client and try and sell your recruitment. Please don't get me wrong I'm not saying it doesn't work, I'm suggesting that if you were to use cold calling as well as the new methods for getting leads you can't help but make more placements and earn more.

Permission marketing was introduced by the Internet marketing pioneer, *Seth Godin*. His argument is as stark and had an almost revolutionary effect on the Recruitment /Search Firm industry:.

The new model, he argues, is built around **permission.** The challenge for marketers is to persuade consumers to volunteer attention - to 'raise their hands' (one of Godin's favourite phrases) - to agree to learn more about a company and its products. *"Permission marketing turns strangers into friends and friends into loyal customers,"* he says. *"It's not just about entertainment - it's about education."*

So, to use this for your marketing efforts, recruiters obtain permission before advancing to the next step in the purchasing process. For example, they ask **permission** to send emails, newsletters, CDs or something of high-perceived value to prospective customers

How this applies to YOUR Recruitment Business:

There are four main reasons why your clients don't buy from you:

1. They don't know you

2. They don't like you

3. They have no need for your services

4. They don't trust you

Which make sense really, would you buy from a firm you had never heard of, don't know, had no need for, didn't like or trust?

Of course not!

So why would you expect your clients to? For some recruiters, if you're new or not sure of your niche, this can be challenging.

So please hold onto your hats, leave your cynicism and negativity outside the office. Turn the phone off, shut down your computer and spend some time discovering what your successful competitors are doing, so that when you do it will increase your earnings and give you more security and fulfilment.

The good news is once you read this and implement it into your business; your business will be one of the few who are doing these things.

The most effective methods for acquiring clients and never ever making another cold call

Just for a moment imagine walking into your office first thing in the morning, then taking a look at your 'to-do list' and on the list there are ten clients that want you to call, so they can discuss their small business needs with you.

For your information, your competitors are in that fortunate situation right now. They never ever make a cold call to a complete stranger begging for the business.

Of course the other advantage when you get this and incorporate it into your business, is that you and your consultants can choose who you work with. If a client is not prepared to pay your fees, you no longer have to compromise yourself or the business. You know that you can generate warm leads every month easily and effortlessly, meaning that you work with your clients on a 'win-win' basis. Once you get this you'll appreciate there is an abundance of clients waiting to work with you.

In total there are 30 effective routes to market, the truth is there are more, but these ten are the most effective.

When you ask the Recruitment/Search Firm Owners who are just doing OK, how they typically acquire new clients the response is 'word of mouth' or 'telephone.' There's nothing wrong with that, if you're generating 30 leads per month every month.

It has been found that the most successful Recruitment/Search Firm Owner uses at least eight routes to market to acquire fee-paying clients. Let me share these routes to market with you, and then we will go into more detail for each one.

For each of the methods I'm about to share with you, you'll never ever have to make another cold call again, and that is a promise.

1. Direct Mail
2. E-Shots
3. Website
4. Pay-per-click and Search Engine Optimization
5. Social Media (LinkedIn, Twitter & Facebook)
6. Remarketing
7. Joint Venture/Strategic Allegiance Host Beneficiary
8. Systemize referral system
9. Thought Leadership
10. Public Relations

If you were to use each of these methods outlined, and only generated five leads on average per method per month, you would generate 50 leads per month. If your conversion rate was only 10% that would mean you would be acquiring five new clients a month every month.

Don't let the fear of the new or the unknown put you off. I've seen Recruitment and Search Firms using these techniques and strategies myself and can personally vouch for their effectiveness.

So you know how many clients you want to work with, you have a well-defined market. Once you know that you can decide how much you want to earn. Yes I did say decide, since success is a choice whether you like it or not!

Whatever you're earning right now, that's your choice. The good news is as you make the choice you decide what you want to earn.

1. Direct Mail

You have options, so first consider your budget and discover your options with the help of your coach and a mailing company.

Next, think about the objective for your client contact. Do you want to focus on a limited-time discount on a service or offer of a report/eBook? With such a targeted focus, a postcard or flyer with punchy copy would suffice.

One of my clients specializes in recruiting accountants. She will send out postcards offering a free eBook such as, *'How to attract the top performing accountants.'*

For every 1000 postcards she sends out, she will get 20 requests for the eBook, and of those 20, at least one of them will lead to a job order, and the others she nurtures over an eight week period, another three will sign up within 12 weeks.

Let's do the calculation on this formula.

To send 1000 post cards at 50p per card, equates to £500. Each one of her clients is worth £6000 in permanent placement fees. So typically she generates £12,000 in 6 months.

2. E-Shots

This is a very similar technique to the direct mailing mentioned above. Again offering the eBook and then nurturing.

The two main differences are, first of all there is no cost to get the eShot out. However, it is worth remembering that the opening rates can be as low as 15%. Consequently if you send out a 1000 emails, only 150 of these emails actually get opened and read. If we work on the same percentage that requested the eBook from the direct mail, that's 3 requesting the book.

Of course the secret here is to email to a larger number, thus increasing your return.

3. Website

One of the big misconceptions is that the key to success is getting traffic. That in my opinion is one of the biggest myths. Look, it's not that difficult to drive traffic to any site, but does that really matter? The answer is no, the key is capturing details of visitors that visit YOUR site and get permission to market to them.

Here are some interesting statistics, less than 1% of those potential clients that visited your site actually buy from it. Can you appreciate the scandal of that; the visitors to your site are at the very least slightly interested in your Recruitment Service, yet at best only 1% actually buy.

If you can get it to say 20%, think of the results that would bring to your profits.

But here is the rub, the way we use the Internet i.e. surfing the net, is that we view a site and then go onto the next site. On average 50% of visitors will make a decision on whether to stay on YOUR website within 8 seconds. So if you have a thirty page website you have a problem.

How to generate leads from your website

Let's say you recruit IT professionals.

When a visitor comes to your website, where would you detail all the types of IT recruitment that you do? One way to overcome this is to have separate landing pages for the different types of IT professionals.

The reason behind this is called Google relevance. The more relevant your landing page is to the search that visitors type into Google, the more easily you'll be found. So if the visitor is looking for a SAP consultant, then your page needs to talk about the benefits of using you to find a SAP consultant.

You have two options as to how to handle a visitor to your site. Your site must have a very clear purpose, so that you can measure the results and be clear of the desired outcome you wish to achieve.

The foundation of all effective marketing is *testing and measuring.* So test and measure results, once you have ascertained what works you can scale up your marketing to get more leads and make more placements.

It is important at this stage that we agree what is an effective website strategy.

There is this myth that once visitors come to your site they will buy. As you have already become aware that does not happen for recruiters, and why should it. Why on earth would someone visit your site and then spend, say £8500, with a stranger.

We now take that concept further and look at lead generation marketing and why long-term it helps us realize the full potential of your marketing.

Your prospects have an unspoken question in their mind: *"Why should I do business with you and not your competitors?"*

And because we want their business, we will do better if we demonstrate our value to them first, before we ask them to spend money with us.

We do this by offering something of value to them in exchange for their contact details (e.g. name, email address) and ask permission to send them marketing messages.

How effective is this?

After collecting the names and email addresses of your potential clients, you now have a database to communicate to on a regular basis (e.g. five times a week). You'll then offer these potential clients free information that's of value to them. By regularly communicating with them with different valuable information such as a free eBook, your database will move from being cold to warm (i.e. move from being a stranger to people who know you really well).

Case studies have shown that sales have increased significantly when contacting a warm database, compared to contacting a cold database. So building your database and nurturing them first before selling to them has proved very effective. But this all begins with you setting up a **landing page** to capture the contact details of your potential clients.

What is a Landing Page?

A landing page, (also called a squeeze page or an opt in page), is a website that has a sign up box on it where potential clients will enter their information, usually their name and email address for a free item, such as an eBook or report.

A splash page is a very short sales page with a link to take the visitor to a landing page or their main website.

The objective of any of these pages, is to get the visitors contact details, such as name and email address, because once you have that information, you can then have a follow up process (usually in the form of regular emails, letters and phone calls) to nurture the relationship with the client who has indicated an interest in your service.

Successful tips for landing pages:

- ✓ Have a compelling headline; remember you have approximately 8 seconds to grab your visitor's attention. If the top half of the web page is empty or has your logo, it is a waste of space.

- ✓ Convey the benefits in the copy. In other words what's

in it for the customer/candidate i.e. Finding top performing consultants, reduce cost per hire, save time etc. Your customer has no interest in your history or your years of experience or your mission statement. A great rule for writing copy is to use the word YOU.

✓ Credibility and Testimonials. Cialdini talks about this in his book: Influence Science and Practice (you can see why I'm such a fan of his book!)

✓ Long copy when selling, short copy when capturing details.

✓ Fancy graphics tend to alienate visitors.

✓ Guarantees increase sales by as much as 40%.

✓ Remember as visitors read your copy, they're having a conversation with themselves, guide the conversation and answer the questions the visitors will be asking.

✓ Put contact details i.e. landline phone number and full address. There are a percentage of visitors that will not engage if there are no contact details.

✓ Build relationships. Start a relationship before you sell to potential clients by giving them something of high value that will enhance your credibility so that they will eventually want to buy from you - this is permission marketing.

✓ Offer a free report, e-book or top tips as valuable content.

✓ Offer a free CD or video in exchange for a prospect's contact details. The higher the perceived value, the greater number will sign up.

✓ Free consultation example *'How to reduce cost per hire'* telephone meeting.

✓ Remember test and measure. So test video, audio graphics etc. There is a great tool on www.audiogenerator.com for putting audio online.

- ✓ Bullet points are the most effective ways of detailing benefits and they're easy on the eye.

- ✓ Show that you respect privacy by telling your prospects that you will not pass their details on.

- ✓ Rather than use the word *'submit'* use a *'send me my free report'* button.

- ✓ Perfection doesn't exist, so just do it, whilst testing and measuring your results.

- ✓ Test how many contact details to ask for. The more information you ask for, the lower the conversion. So if you ask for full name address, phone number and email address, your opt-in rates are reduced. However tests have shown that those that are prepared to give more information tend to be better quality leads. Again, test and measure.

- ✓ A squeeze/landing page is where you simply ask for the name, email address and telephone number, no more, no less. Generally it has no other links and only has two options - sign up and provide details or go away.

- ✓ Tests have shown giving visitors less choice improves opt-in rates.

- ✓ There are some stories around that Google does not like squeeze pages. This is not true, as long as you offer something of value and relevance there is no problem.

- ✓ Also use video, as Google owns YouTube so this helps with getting you ranked higher in search results. *Examples "Go to my PC" and "Confused.com"*

- ✓ Evidence has shown that once visitors click on your page once, they're likely to click on another page.

Often we are told that this won't work for our recruitment sector. That it's not true from a personal point of view, I have recruitment clients who have increased sales by 80% in 6 months simply by using 'permission marketing' effectively. What I can guarantee is you'll get more leads than you're currently getting.

Be aware of the above the line and below the line. This is where the visitors have to scroll down the page; it is a very important part. If your visitors have to scroll down to read, then you're losing visitors.

It is always possible to improve the performance of your landing page, by using split testing.

Here are the top tips you must do to generate leads via your website.

- Only 4% of the visitors to your site are ready to buy

- Buyers have become more sophisticated and are likely to do some research prior to purchase of your small business service

- 93% of small business owners don't generate any leads via their website

- 97% of small business owners don't follow up more than 4 times

- 81% of potential buyers don't make a purchase until after the 5th contact

This means a lot of small business owners are losing clients to the top performing small business owner, who knows how to nurture potential clients.

This is what the top performing small business owners are doing:

1. Establish how many visitors you're getting now, by installing Google analytics, this is free software that measure many things about your website, including the number of visitors, average time spend on your site, what pages visitors look at, how visitors found your site

and so much more invaluable information.

2. Get a basic understanding of keyword density to move your site up Google search.

3. Make the copy on your website benefit led. In other words explain what you'll do for them. If you use the word *"we"*, *"our"*, *"your company name"* and any reference about you then you're driving traffic away.

4. Follow the basic website copy rules **A.I.D.A**. So first capture visitors **ATTENTION**, then get them **INTERESTED** then create **DESIRE** followed by **ACTION** asking them to call you, email you or request a free report.

5. Create a free report on your site such as *'7 questions you should ask a Recruitment/Search Firm before you engage them'* ask for their details in return for the free report.

6. Constantly drive visitors to your website.

An example of this:

One of my clients operates in the hospitality sector. Using the lead capture form (How to find the top staff for your hotel) on her website, she generates 50 leads per month. Her typical conversion is two per month every month. Her clients typically spend £4700 per transaction.

Again you do the math!

But seriously, it's not just the financial reward; it's the fact she never calls a client unless the client has indicated they're looking to recruit.

When one of her prospects downloads her client magnet, this is indicating to her that they're interested in what she has to offer and they're giving her 'permission' to market her services to them.

4. Pay per Click (PPC)

Pay Per Click is an Online marketing model used to direct traffic to websites, where you pay the hosting service (such as Google, LinkedIn or Facebook) when the advert is clicked. The beauty of this is you only pay when someone clicks on your advert. You can also set a weekly budget and once that has been met, then the advertising stops. This means you're controlling your marketing spend.

Pay Per Click is a great way to drive targeted prospects to your website, but in order for this to work, you need to test and measure results to make sure you're getting a return on your investment.

Here is an example of generating leads using LinkedIn PPC:

One of my clients recruits in the automotive sector worldwide for senior engineering staff. Using LinkedIn PPC he has requested that his advert is only seen by MD, HRD and Chief Engineers in the automotive industry. His advert is for a report called *"How to reduce your cost per hire in the automotive sector."*

From this he generates fifty to seventy leads per month with a conversion rate of 5%. Since his average fee is $9,400. This one method generates $23,000 per month every month or $282,000 per year.

5. Social Media (LinkedIn, Twitter & Facebook)

In my opinion, Social Media is one of the fastest growing and successful marketing strategies for Recruitment/Search Firm owners with a return on investment that can't be rivalled.

To implement a successful Social Media marketing strategy takes little financial investment. However, it does require relentless time commitment, not only to make it work, but to maximize its effectiveness. In order to be successful, you need to keep up with and manage your effort over time, without neglecting other important areas of your business.

In order to be a successful marketer, you need to engage your audience and communicate with them through several mediums. Social Media allows you to do this, whilst building your network and directing targeted traffic to your website and landing pages.

Once you have successfully implemented this marketing strategy into your business, you can expect to generate an additional ten to fifteen leads per month, every month, just by using this route to market alone!

Before you begin, you need to know that there are literally hundreds of social media platforms out there, so it's important to only invest your time in the ones that get you the best results.

Our research has found that there are currently 3 social media sites that give recruiters the best return in terms of time invested.

- ✓ LinkedIn
- ✓ Twitter
- ✓ Facebook

LinkedIn

LinkedIn is the world's largest professional network with over 227 million members and growing rapidly. LinkedIn connects you to your trusted contacts and helps you exchange knowledge, ideas, and opportunities with a broader network of professionals.

Let me ask you a question...

Since there are 227 million members on LinkedIn, do you think it is possible that your potential clients are on there waiting to hear from you?

You see we work with a number of top performing small business owners who only use LinkedIn to attract clients.

Here is an example of generating leads through LinkedIn:

One of our clients recruits in the energy conservation sector. So he created a group on LinkedIn for professionals on that sector. In less than three months he was the owner of the largest group in that sector on LinkedIn. He sends his group members high value content every month. He drives them to his website to get the material, and guess what, every month at least 4 potential clients ask if he can contact them regarding small business.

For every four inquiries, two become clients every month. This equates to £15,000 per month or £180,000 per year.

Twitter

Twitter is a website, owned and operated by Twitter Inc., which offers a social networking and micro blogging service, enabling its users to send and read messages called tweets. Tweets are based on text posts of up to 140 characters.

*Some interesting facts about Twitter according to –
www.digitalbuzzblog.com*

- There are over 106 million active Twitter accounts

- The number of Twitter users increases by approximately 300,000 per day

- Twitter users are sending over 55 million tweets per day

So, imagine if just 0.01% of Twitter users were in your target market. If one of your competitors implemented Twitter into their marketing strategy and you didn't. Who do you think would generate the most leads, communicate to the most prospects and sign the most clients?

An example of how to generate leads using Twitter:

One of my clients recruits in the medical sector; she opened an account and started to follow the decision makers and key players in her field. About 40% of those she followed then followed her.

She would then send personal messages to decision makers to engage them and position herself as an authority in that field. Please note at no time does she post vacancies or sell. She also offered a report on 'How to write an advert to attract the top nurses?' This is posted once a week and every week she gets 1% of her 1200 followers requesting the report, which is approximately twelve leads per month. With the clients she has sent a direct message to, she will call and arrange a meeting, for every 5 meetings she gets one vacancy.

Facebook

Some interesting facts about Facebook:

- There are more than 750 million active users
- 50% of our active users log on to Facebook in any given day
- People spend over 700 billion minutes per month on Facebook

So what do these interesting facts and figures mean to you as a Recruitment/Search Firm Owner? To put it quite simply, there are a mass of potential clients waiting to hear from you on these social media platforms, with the added benefit that it is relatively easy to target your niche.

If you're not currently using social media, in my opinion you're losing out on revenue for your business. You see marketing is very much a numbers game. The more people you communicate to, the more leads you'll get and the more clients you'll acquire.

Social Media is a great, cost-effective way to communicate to your target market.

6. Remarketing

Remarketing is a feature that lets you reach clients and candidates who have previously visited your website, but did not call you or engage with you

You can now show them relevant adverts across the web or when they search on Google. When people leave your site without engaging with you, remarketing helps you connect with these potential clients and candidates again. You can even show them a tailored message or offer that will encourage them to return to your site and request further information or contact you.

Use remarketing to match the right message to the right people at the right time. Here's how: You add a piece of code (remarketing tag) to all of the pages of your site. Then, when a client or candidate comes to your site, they'll be added to your remarketing lists. You can later connect with these potential buyers while they search on Google or browse other websites.

From the client and candidate's point of view, it seems that you're everywhere. The best bit is, if you do it on Pay per `click you only pay if they're interested and click on your advert.

Many companies are using this right now, and more and more Recruitment companies are enjoying huge success with this method.

One of our clients reported a 33% increase in opt in conversion when they implemented this into their marketing.

7. Joint Venture/Strategic Allegiance Host Beneficiary

This method is considered one of the most powerful ways to attract warm leads, when you and your business implement this system and systemize the procedure you'll have:

✓ More clients

✓ Generate more income

✓ Increase turnover

✓ Have greater security for you and your family

This method of lead generation has been a marketing method for holiday companies, mail order companies, newspapers and magazines and numerous online businesses.

A Joint Venture takes on many forms, such as asking a company that sells to the same market as you if they would email their list informing their clients of your service. In return the company will expect some form of reimbursement typically a percentage of invoice value, or a reciprocal arrangement.

Whatever deal you agree, whenever you approach a 'host' company you should endeavor to extend a special offer to his/her clients. This maybe in the form of extended warranty, free bonus or even reduced price.

Why Joint Ventures work so well:

Have you ever called a cold prospect? It can be at times tedious and some of my clients find it nerve-racking at the thought of rejection.

✓ Joint Ventures allow you to leverage off the credibility of others.

✓ Did you know it is 500% easier to get an existing client to buy than it is to persuade a new client to purchase?

✓ It positions the host in a positive light. The business owner is recommending a service that benefits his/her clients, and the clients appreciate that he/she is looking out for them.

✓ You can reciprocate and generate money for your business.

✓ It is virtually risk free

One of my clients recently bought a Recruitment franchise and with the monthly investment he has to make to the franchise owner, it was imperative his business hit the ground running.

Well the first thing he did was get himself a coach to ensure that he did what he said he was going to do. He explained to us that he had no database of potential clients and wanted the fastest and most effective method for growing his small business. We shared with him the *"Don't sell to, sell through"*

Let me explain. The Recruitment Owner arranged meetings with 23 accountancy firms in his town and then made the following offer to them:

"I will recruit for you completely free for one position; on the understanding that once you see how this benefits you, you'll then introduce my Recruitment Firm to your B2B clients." Of the 43 he spoke too, <u>seven took up the offer immediately.</u>

Look at it from the accountant's point of view, they have nothing to lose. This recruiter went from zero income to £180k pa in 12 months, using only that method. In his second year he took on two other consultants, as he was unable to cope with the leads he was getting. Again none of his team ever makes a cold call.

8. The Systemized Referral Process System

When you have this in place, properly in place, then you'll get some remarkable benefits.

To start with you can obtain hundreds, yes, hundreds of low cost or even 'no cost' leads.

✓ Referrals tend to have a higher conversion rate than any other type of lead.

✓ You have satisfied customers/candidates. People only provide referrals when they're satisfied with the products and services they're receiving.

✓ You'll experience increased turnover and profits and whatever benefits you get as a result of those increases.

✓ You'll acquire assignments through the referral route rather than through cold sales.

✓ You'll have the opportunity to reduce your marketing spend.

✓ You'll lock in current clients to you.

✓ You'll have reduced acquisition cost per customer.

These are some of the great benefits from getting referrals and the only real way to do it, to get all of these advantages, is to have a systemized process.

Without a doubt, referrals can be the least expensive capture cost leads we ever receive.

Often, referrals can be obtained at no cost. However, should a cost be associated, it would be on a contingency basis. That is, payment would only be necessary for converted business or new clients and not just for the leads.

Earlier I mentioned that a lot of Recruitment/Search Firm business owners often say they get the business via 'word of mouth/referral.' However when you dig deeper, we often discover that they have not systemized the process and they get very few.

Here is an example from a Recruitment Owner who works only with blue chip organizations such as Proctor and Gamble and other FMCG organizations, recruiting their sales teams.

Due to the nature of the small business her company does, she tends to work with the sales director and sales manager. She has incorporated a very simple system that means once an assignment has been completed, and the client is extremely satisfied, she asks them a series of very precise questions. Each time she does this she gets between 4-10 leads!

Her conversion rate is 8% (that maybe needs working on) each client is worth £8000 p.a. and over a lifetime about £40,000. Again this is her only method for getting business. She has a thriving small business that turns over in excess of £750,000 per year.

By simply asking the right questions to the right people, she never ever makes a cold call.

9. Thought Leadership

In your industry there are always 'Key People of Influence':

- Their names come up in conversation ... for all the right reasons

- They attract opportunities ... the right sort

- They earn more money ... and it isn't a struggle

- Clients go to them

Key People enjoy a special status in their chosen field because they're well connected, well known, well regarded and highly valued. These KPIs or 'Go to' people tend to earn more and work less.

All the previous techniques and strategies discussed will help position you as a KPI, there are only 3 things missing and they are:

1. Become an author in the field that you recruit in. (I know a great writing coach!)

2. Become a public speaker in your field. This can be done live at seminars or via virtual seminars such as webinars.

3. Have a compelling 'Elevator Statement'; a statement that defines who you are and what you do for your

clients that can be delivered in the time it would take you to take an average elevator ride 10 floors .

An example of this:

One of my clients is a rec-to-rec recruiter in the USA. He actually uses nine routes to market. The consequence of which, is he is able to generate eighty leads per month every month. He would expect to acquire eight new clients a month every month, his business turnover is just over $2m per year and he works four days per week.

He is invited to sit on panels, and speaks at most of the major events in the industry; he has more clients coming to him than any other recruiter that we work with.

10. Public Relations

The beauty of PR is it's FREE! It lets you reach your target market people. It can also make you famous and people will start recognizing you as you go about your business.

Think about this for a minute, you're flicking through a local newspaper and you come to the classified adverts. Here you see the typical ads such as 'man with a van' or the gardening service etc. You then flick to the next page where you start to read an article about a business who specializes in recruiting senior IT professionals. The small business company has just released a report *'How to attract the best IT professional'*. The article then goes on to give a brief description of the report and a bit about the business.

Is it possible that if you were a client looking to recruit IT professionals that this report would be of interest to you, and you would probably request the report? Is it also possible that because this article is not an advert you're more likely to believe it?

One of my clients who recruits in the retail sector in the USA is able to use this method extremely effectively. He has a monthly column in a retail magazine that's distributed to his target market. He's generating 10 leads per month, equally important, he drives traffic to his website and is seen as a KPI within the retail recruiting sector.

Being outstanding at marketing is fairly straightforward – but so few Recruitment Business Owners do it.

There is one caveat that I must add to what I have shared with you. You must continually test these new marketing strategies on a small scale. It may be a new direct mail campaign, a new advert, a letter to your customers, an email, a new headline on your website. You test small, and then you measure the results. What did it cost? What revenue did it generate? If it wasn't profitable you've learnt an important lesson – move on. If it was profitable, you roll it out and make it an integral part of your marketing mix.

I appreciate that we've shared a lot with you and you're now sitting there excited at the potential, but at the same time, you may be a little overwhelmed.

Can I also share with you that none of the examples given here were from small business owners with a super intellect, or maybe a background in marketing, none of them would call themselves super sales people. You've probably noticed from the examples given, in most cases the clients went to them.

That's the beauty of effective marketing, when your target market raise their hands and say, *"I could be interested in the service your business provides."*

So to summarize there are several ways you can generate leads without making cold calls. It is estimated that when you use *'Permission Marketing'* to generate leads, between 5%-15% of those leads/inquiries are 'now buyers' on other words you'll get a job order from them in the next two to eight weeks.

Action Steps

Einstein defined insanity as *"Doing what you have always done and expecting different results."*

If you're not happy and content with the results you're currently getting, then it is time to do something different, because nothing is going to change until you make that decision and decide to do things differently.

1. What is the main problem that your prospects are facing right now? Find this, and you have your prospects' need.

2. How can you resolve this problem? Answer this, and you have a solution to their need.

3. What's the best form of presenting this solution to your prospects? Is it a report or an eBook etc.? Answer this, and you have your bait to reel them in.

4. Create the bait, using attention-grabbing copy.

5. Create a landing page with the same attention-grabbing copy. It should be a summary using bullet points to highlight key benefits. Include a form for prospects to fill in their contact details in exchange for the free e-Book.

6. Create an email promoting the eBook, again with attention-grabbing copy with a link to your landing page.

7. Finally send out the email and measure your results.

To get some **FREE** examples of reports that Recruitment and Search Firms have used successfully, simply go to www.drewcoaching.com/sevendeadlythreats to download them.

Remember! You can always create new baits relevant to your prospect's different needs.

Deadly Threat #6
Not Having Effective
Time Management

Deadly Threat # 6
Not Having Effective Time Management

"What is important is seldom urgent and what is urgent is seldom important."
President Dwight D. Eisenhower

Have YOU got a minute?

Ever wonder what separates the very best of the best? Lots of people would point to genetics, education, economic climate, or the sector they operate in. But usually, those parts aren't as big as you might think...

Imagine that 86,400 of your local currency is deposited into your bank account. It's 100% legal and you're free to do whatever you want with the money. The only catch is, at the end of the day, whatever's left of the 86,400 gets taken away from you and you lose out.

So what do you do? Well... Anyone with an ounce of sanity would make that most of every last penny! Wouldn't you?

Think about what you would do, if you had 86,400 to spend each day....

So, what's the point?

Well... every day you're given exactly 86,400 seconds. You can do whatever you want with the time, but at the end of the day, whatever time you've not made the most of gets taken away from you and you never get it back.

The thing about we humans is... *we're procrastinators!*

We put things off and we put things off some more, until it eventually gets to the point where we have nothing more to put off other than 'putting things off' itself. The big frustration isn't 'not knowing what the solution is', it's the 'not getting round to doing it' that holds most of us back.

In my opinion there is no such thing as time management; to be effective you must *manage yourself.*

Below will help you calculate what your time is worth:

Target Income	⇨	**A**
Working days in a year	⇨	235
Hours in a working day	⇨	**C** 7
Working hours in a year	⇨	**D** 1645
A /D = Your hourly worth (before deductions)	⇨	**E**

Doing this exercise will really help put your time into perspective. It's also worth considering that the average person is effective for between 25 minutes to four hours per day.

Most Recruitment/Search Firm Business Owners have no idea where the time goes. This in turn leads to frustration as you can spend ten to twelve hours a day working, yet feel as if you haven't achieved much. Being reactive often causes this.

Common causes of this are:

- ✓ Candidates calling you unexpectedly
- ✓ Your email
- ✓ Clients calling you unexpectedly
- ✓ Your mobile phone
- ✓ Unplanned meetings
- ✓ YOU
- ✓ Internet
- ✓ Social media

How to overcome this:

You now know what your time is worth in hard cash, and you have identified the time thieves. So, now what?

A Time Audit

For the next ten days, be absolutely honest with yourself and record exactly where you spend your time by keeping a time audit. In this audit, include every single thing that you do, including traveling, looking up the sports results on the web and the time you spend on Facebook.

Below is an example of what your time audit sheet could look like.

TIME AUDIT SHEET		
Time	Activity	Enough/not enough time?
8:00 - 8:30		
8:30 - 9:00		
9:00 - 9:30		
9:30 - 10:00		
10:00 - 10:30		
10:30 - 11:00		
11:00 - 11:30		
11:30 - 12:00		
12:00 - 12:30		
12:30 - 1:00		
1:00 - 1:30		
1:30 - 2:00		
2:00 - 2:30		
2:30 - 3:00		
3:00 - 3:30		
3:30 - 4:00		
4:00 - 4:30		
4:30 - 5:00		

Time Analysis

Upon completion of audit, identify where if you're spending too much, or perhaps too little time on tasks.

Then answer these questions:

- *When are you most productive?*
- *What do you do most every day that will take you closer to achieving your goal?*
- *Does your analysis reflect that?*
- *If you had more time what would you do?*
- *If you had less time what would you do?*
- *What areas of your life is procrastination a problem for you?*

Strategies used by the Top Recruitment/Search Firm Business Owners:

1. **Having a well-defined goal.** By having a well-defined goal you know exactly where you and your business are going and what precisely you must do to get there. This helps you prioritize what needs to be done. A question to ask is 'what 3 things must I do today that will take me closer to my goal?' Once your priorities have been established you'll have the clarity. Remember this doesn't only apply to your business life but also to your personal life

2. **Delegation.** The only way you'll get everything done, is by delegating that task that can be delegated, this applies to the Recruitment Owner with a team of 100 and the sole trader.

   There are numerous tasks that can be outsourced.

   Outsourcing/Virtual admin support

   ➲ www.odesk.com/-

- ➲ https://www.elance.com/
- ➲ http://www.freelancer.com/work/market-research-india/
- ➲ http://www.peopleperhour.com/freelance/virtual+pa+lifestyle+assistant
- ➲ http://www.talentgurus.net/virtual-assistant.html

3. **Discover the secret to saying NO!** It really easy to get into the habit of saying yes to everything. An example of this is: The client that gives you a lot of business then asks you to fill a role that you have no expertise or experience in. You believe it is better to say yes rather than let your competitors do it. That's so wrong!

   The top firms have a well-defined goal and know how they're going to get there. If they're asked to do something that will not take them closer to their goal then the answer is a resounding NO!

Create a Timeline

Once you have decided on what needs to be done, set a timeline. A goal without a timeline is a 'wish' so schedule time for everything:

- ➲ Contacting candidates
- ➲ Contacting clients
- ➲ Writing proposals
- ➲ Following up on leads
- ➲ Interviewing candidates
- ➲ Internal/external meetings
- ➲ Admin.
- ➲ Creating to-do list

⮑ Family time.

Make a Decision

The most successful Recruitment and Search Firm Business Owners have the ability to make a decision. It has been found that indecisiveness creates stress for the person that's being indecisive. Clearly communicate your expectations to your team.

One of the biggest time robbers is 'miscommunication'. Whenever you say or think 'I didn't mean it like that,' this is a sign you haven't communicated your expectations clearly and precisely.

There is no such thing as an inflexible client, candidate, consultant, friend, or partner, just an inflexible communicator.

If you were to accept that presumption then you would take responsibility for the outcome, and it gets you to look at your communication style.

Just some of the benefits of systemizing your business;

- ✓ More time
- ✓ More money
- ✓ Business works if you're there or not
- ✓ More valuable – a business with documented workable systems is worth far more than a business that has no systems
- ✓ Easier to take your business to the next level – franchise, license, public float or sell.

Systemize every aspect of your business

As mentioned before, management is closely linked to effective communications. Numerous studies have shown that the most successful Recruitment and Search Firms systemize every single aspect of their business, which means firstly, your staff does not have to reinvent the wheel for each task to be done.

A good example of this is McDonalds Restaurants;

Whatever your personal opinion of them, you know that wherever in the world you are, when visiting a McDonalds, the food and the service is consistent

The reason is quite simple; everything is systemized. From the way you're greeted to how the staff always 'up sell' you to the larger size, to the fact that regardless of what the temperature is outside you're always given ice whether you ask for it or not (this, by the way, saves McDonalds millions of dollars every year).

Imagine if your Recruitment Business could run without you there? That's what systems can do for your business. Every member of staff knows exactly what they need to do and when, and every task is handled the same way, cutting down on problems.

Systemizing your business will give you a very good idea of the flow of information or activity within your business. It allows you, the owner to go on holidays and know everything will be done as it should be. When new people join your team there will be a manual they can follow. There will be consistency in all activities.

Systemizing your business can be as simple as documenting all daily, weekly or monthly activities each employee needs to do. This can be done by writing them down, or possibly photographing, or capturing them on video or audio CD.

Action Steps

- Sit down with your team, and come up with a way to start documenting what they do. Then start to compile it into a 'Systems' folder.

- Create a Time Audit sheet (as described on page 95) and fill it out.

- Get everyone into the habit of documenting even the smallest things, from how to answer the telephone, to how to follow up a client.

- Get someone to collate all of the information and keep it in one place, then regularly update it.

If you need extra help with your *systemizing*, then visit www.drewcoaching.com/sevendeadlythreats for additional tools and resources that will help you implement this into your business.

Deadly Threat # 7
Not Knowing What You *Should* Know

"You've got to think winter in the summer. It's just too easy to get faked out when the sky is blue and the clouds are fleecy. You've got to prepare for winter because it's coming, it always does."
Jim Rohn

Deadly Threat # 7
Not Knowing What You *Should* Know

"The highest form of ignorance is when you reject something you don't know anything about."
Wayne Dyer

The fact is, if you came into this business believing that if you get really good at the sourcing, placing candidates and meeting the clients' needs, then you'll experience untold success, money and fame, then you're sadly mistaken.

The honest truth is, you could be the best recruiter with the finest consultants, you could have the largest database of candidates in the world, your fees could be the lowest in the universe, however, unless you have clients you have not got a business.

Now don't get me wrong, you do need to know and understand the fundamentals of Recruitment and Search Firms, and you really need to offer a competitive and reliable services.

But it's your marketing and sales that really drive your business success. That's why it is imperative you have a proven and effective method for attracting clients and candidates.

If you don't have a tried and tested method for attracting clients and candidates to your business, then you're at the mercy of your clients methods of buying, or more likely not buying, your Recruitment Services.

I remember once asking a client what his Average Placement Value (APV) and Life Time Value (LTV) was (I kind of made the assumption that every Recruitment Business Owners would have those numbers to hand, and if not, could quickly put their hands on them). His response left me dumbfounded and shocked, because he simply said, *"I have absolutely no idea and I wouldn't even know how to get them."*

Now for those of you not familiar with the terminology, please let me explain. If you're a perm recruiter, look at all your placements over the last two years, and total the amount, then divide that by the number of placements. That would give you your Average Placements Value (APV). If you were a temp./contract firm, the figure you would require is the average hourly profit you made on each contractor/temp. out

The Life Time Value means, once a client gives you the first assignment that's usually just the beginning and you're likely to get more placements over the duration of the relationship. So for a perm recruiter you may get, say four placements over the lifetime of that relationship, and if each placement is worth 10k then the LTV is 4x10 = 40k.

Please bear with me, even if the thought of doing the numbers is causing your brain to hurt, the reason these numbers are so important to you is, unless you know the average value of your clients, how on earth are you going to know how much to invest to acquire a client?

Here is a question I get asked at least once a week...

"How much should I budget for my marketing to attract clients and grow my business?"

In my opinion that's the **wrong question**. The question you should ask is

"How much am I prepared to invest to acquire/buy clients to grow my business?"

Let me explain.

Let's say that you're a perm. recruiter and your average placement is 10k and your LTV is 40k of your local currency. That means that on average, every new client is worth 40K.

And let's say you decide to embark on a Pay Per Click (PPC) campaign to get new business, and you decide to use LinkedIn PPC as this is a good source for leads. At the moment LinkedIn PPC is more expensive than Google, Bing and certainly

Facebook, however the quality of the leads tends to be better, so you're paying 20 pounds or dollars per lead via LinkedIn.

Let me ask you a question.

If every time you gave me 2000 of your local currency, and I gave you 40k in return, when would you stop giving me 2000 of your currency?

Silly question really!

Because you wouldn't, I mean why would you...?

Well, if you're paying 20 dollars or pounds per lead on LinkedIn PPC to get 100 leads, it will cost you 2k of your local currency, and let's say you only converted 1% of those 100 leads, that could be worth 40k (and you've got to admit, a 1% conversion is pretty lousy, but 20 times return of you investment is pretty good!).

If you wanted an additional 400k in placements on the numbers above, that would be a 20,000k investment in LinkedIn PPC, and if you only converted 1% of those leads it would give you an additional 400,000!

Wouldn't that end your sleepless nights? Wouldn't that end the worry about your underperforming consultants? Wouldn't that mean an end to the famine and feast situation you're currently enduring? Wouldn't that take away any doubt or insecurity you're feeling right now?

With those numbers you now have a business that's scalable, predictable and sellable. You know how much you need to invest to get 40k or 400k. Just think about that for a minute.

How to Manage The Sales Process, to Make More Placements and Create a Business of Value

There is a myth that no doubt you'll hear a million times; 'Great recruiters are born not made', quite frankly that's BS!

Selling and delivery Recruitment assignment is a process. The big mistakes many Recruitment Business Owners make, is they just leave it all to their consultants, and when it goes wrong, and it surely will, the owner then blames the incompetent consultant. Very few Recruitment Business Owners take a long hard look at the part they played in the failure of the consultant.

Let's bake a cake (bear with me on this...)

Consider this, if you were asked to bake a Victoria sponge cake, you would simply follow the recipe. You know that if you follow the process you can almost guarantee the outcome.

Here is the recipe...

The traditional afternoon teacake, named after Queen Victoria, remains a classic – two layers of light sponge, tasting of butter and vanilla, sandwiched with plenty of fruity jam. It looks so simple, so unadorned yet most appealing.

The sponge is made by the 'creaming' method – that's, the butter is creamed or beaten with the sugar, after which the eggs are gradually beaten in and finally the flour is carefully folded into the mixture. Good beating is the key to a good sponge.

To make one large cake

For the sponge:

225g unsalted butter, softened

225g caster sugar

4 large free-range eggs, at room temperature

½ teaspoon vanilla extract

225g self-raising flour

1 tablespoon milk, at room temperature

For the filling:

6 rounded tablespoons good raspberry jam

To finish:

Caster or icing sugar, for dusting

2 x 20.5cm sandwich tins, greased and base-lined

1. Preheat the oven to 180°C/350°F/gas 4. Put the soft butter into a mixing bowl and beat with a wooden spoon, an electric mixer or your hand for a minute until very smooth and creamy.

2. Gradually beat in the sugar, then keep on beating for 3 to 4 minutes or until the mixture turns almost white and becomes very fluffy in texture; scrape down the bowl from time to time. Break the eggs into a small bowl, add the vanilla and beat lightly with a fork just to break them up. Slowly add to the creamed mixture, a tablespoon at a time, giving the mixture a good beating after each addition and frequently scraping down the bowl. This will take about 5 minutes. If the mixture looks as if it is about to curdle add a tablespoon of the sifted flour and then continue adding the last portions of egg. Gently but thoroughly fold the flour into the egg mixture using a large metal spoon. Do this as lightly as possible so you don't knock out the air you have beaten in.

4. Stop folding when there are no streaks of flour visible in the mixture.

5. Spoon the mixture into the 2 tins so they're equally filled – you can do this by eye or by weighing the tins as you fill them.

6. Spread the mixture evenly in the tins, right to the edges.

7. Bake for 20 to 25 minutes or until a good golden brown and the sponges are springy when gently pressed with your fingertip. They should almost double in size during baking.

8. Remove the tins from the oven and leave for a minute – the sponges will contract slightly. Run a round-bladed knife around the inside of each tin to loosen the sponge, then turn out onto

a wire rack and leave to cool.

9. Set one sponge upside down on a serving platter and spread over the jam. Gently set the other sponge, golden crust up, on top. Dust with sugar.

Store in an airtight container and eat within 5 days.

Well guess what, *the same applies to the Recruitment process.*

Not the Victoria Sponge, but having a well-defined system and process for your team to follow, so that when they do, you can easily predict the results.

However if you were to examine the majority of Recruitment Firms you'll discover that each consultant does things differently, admittedly it may not be vastly different but it is different and what that means to you is inconsistent delivery... and what does that mean to the client and candidates? Inconsistent delivery.

Which means you have an underperforming consultant that's costing you time and money.

It doesn't make senses does it? But for some crazy reason that's what happens in most firms.

If you want to maximize your profits and maximize the performance of your team you must have a well-defined system and process in place, where you know for example;

- How many leads you must generate to achieve your goal
- What your average placement value is
- What the average profit you make on perm/contractors is
- What your LTV is
- How much you spend to generate leads for you and your consultants

- What the conversion rate when you get a lead is
- What the process for following up leads is
- What the process to deliver on the assignment is

If you've got a business that's reliant on <u>you</u> winning the business, and you deliver the Recruitment, then you haven't got a business, you've got a job, and there's a big difference between the two. If you want a business that you can sell, so you can create the lifestyle you truly desire, then the greater the systemization, the greater the value.

Now if you're thinking, well the thought of systems and processes turn me off, I'm with you my friend. Quite frankly, the thought does nothing for me. However, it's the ONLY way you'll be able to create a business rather than a job.

There's a lot of rubbish talked about the spontaneity of the consultants, and not wanting to 'micro-manage,' but the truth of the matter is, <u>if you can't measure it, you can't manage it!</u>

If you're not managing the business and your team, then the business and your team are managing you, and I really don't recommend that!

It never ceases to amaze me the difficulty and challenges that Recruitment Business Owners have in recruiting for their own company. If their clients knew of the problems they were encountering in finding people for themselves, they would never give that Recruitment Company another job order.

The reason for the problems? Unrealistic expectations!

The typical Recruitment/Search Firm Business sets up in business, usually after working for another Recruitment Firm. More often than not, the owner then decides that ALL they have to do is recruit a team of 'Top Billers' and 'happy days'.

So the owner then goes on the lookout for the 'Top Biller' who must possess the following;

1. At least 3 years' experience of that particular sector

2. Evidence of being a 'Top Biller' in their current company

3. The ability to bring business and their network with them

Now wanting those qualities are quite understandable, but ask yourself this question; *Why would a 'Top Biller', who is doing great at their current firm, leave all that to join your new firm, to start from scratch, particularly if coming from the contract/temp sector?*

However, you interview endless number of consultants who all claim to be the 'Top Billers' in their firm, who have now been made redundant.

Just think about that for a moment.

If they really were 'Top billers' and making the company pots of money, why were they made redundant? I'm not saying it is impossible, but it's unlikely.

Anyway after interviewing what seem like millions of consultants all claiming to be 'Top billers', you make an offer and they start working for you. At first all seems well, the enthusiasm and optimism is almost contagious; there is real hope for the business. The new guy rings round all their contacts and old clients. They get told 'nothing at the moment but keep in touch.' The consultant tells you that they have been promised the next job order and looking at their forecast they're likely to bill a million in the first year alone.

After 3 months there are still no placements. It would seem that the consultant's enthusiasm is now waning, the newbie is not calling out as often. They've gone through all their old contacts, and it's normally about this time there's an increase in the amount of time they spend on the computer, doing research and emailing clients and candidates.

In the fourth month the newbie gets a split fee, and you think at last they're now turning the corner. Alas, now into fifth month and the numbers are not looking good, indeed this consultant is costing you money!

You'll then decide one, some or all of the following:

1. It's time to start paying for performance, not just for showing up.

2. Maybe just maybe, next month things will get better.

3. The consultant is a fool and an idiot and clearly isn't what he made out to be I need to cut my loses and get rid.

4. If I get rid I'll be back to where I was, and and my friends and family will question what I'm doing, so I'll give him more time.

By what if you were to do this instead:

1. Create a systemized business that doesn't require you to try and recruit 'Top Billers'. Instead you now recruit individuals who have a certain attitude and a certain amount of intellect. Those two things can be measured using psychometric and IQ questionnaires.

2. You now recruit two trainee consultants at the same time who have the attributes but not necessarily the experience.

3. You systemize every single aspect of your business, from the way the phone is answered to generating the leads. You ban cold calling and promise that you'll give each consultant 50 leads a month every month.

4. Systemise the entire Recruitment process.

The FORTY step Placement/Recruitment Process

1. Take a COMPLETE job order

2. Ask for retainer or exclusive on every role

3. Agree client investment

4. Agree dates with client for interviews, dates for feedback (note if you do not have at least point 4 you DO NOT have a job order and should not work on it)

5. Confirm points 1-4 in writing use template email

6. Create Recruitment Plan using a template

7. Commence file search

8. Gathering appropriate names of candidates

9. Candidate Contact

10. Connect with all candidates via LinkedIn

11. Interview candidates

12. Presentation of Candidate to Employer

13. Set-up First Interview

14. Prepare candidates for interviews

15. Confirm Appointment with Candidate and Employer (Prep Employer)

16. Debrief Candidate

17. Debrief Employer

18. Set Second Interview

19. Reference Check

20. Connect with all references via LinkedIn

21. Offer (Client magnet/eBook) to all references

22. Get at least three leads from references

23. Second Interview, Prep Candidate (Trial Closing)

24. Second Interview, Prep Employer (Trial Closing)

25. Confirm Second Interview with Employer and Candidate

26. Debrief Candidate (Closing)

27. Debrief Employer (Closing)

28. Closing/Negotiating

29. Offer/Acceptance/Start Date

30. Resignation preparation with candidate

31. Agree start date with candidate and client

32. Confirm all in writing with all parties

33. Billing Prep

34. Fill out Billing Information

35. Stay in Touch with Candidate

36. Confirm that the Candidate has started

37. Get paid

38. Stay in touch with candidate for period of guarantee

39. Ask the hiring manager what other skills will be required over the next quarter

40. Get testimonial from client and candidate

Remember what I told you in the previous chapter, about how systemizing everything you do is a really smart way to take your business forward? Well the same can be applied to how you recruit new staff.

So you know if they follow the process you know what the outcome is going to be. A bit like when you go into a McDonalds restaurant and order a coke, burger and fries, you know that wherever in the world you go to get that, it will be consistent.

Other Little Known Threats to YOU and The Recruitment/Search Firm Industries

Some experts claim that the history of Recruitment goes back as far as ancient Egypt. The more popular view is that it really took off after the Second World War.

This is when agencies were formed to help service men and woman back into the world of civilian life and work.

It is estimated that the total industry in English speaking countries is worth $120 billion!

Certainly from my days of the industry, nearly 25 years ago, things have changed and there are certainly more threats to the industry than at any other time in its history.

Here a just a few in no particular order:

> ➤ **The growth of procurement departments is having a negative impact on the industry.** These departments are treating Recruitment as a commodity.

> ➤ **Candidate's searching habits have changed dramatically.** When I worked as a Search consultant the only place to advertise the vacancy was in the National Newspapers and trade journals. Today 87% of job seekers go Online first to find jobs.

> ➤ **Balancing the global and the local** – managing, hiring and identifying talent globally while retaining important local insights.

> ➤ **Managing a flexible and virtual workforce** – but not at the cost of loyalty and career development.

> ➤ **Retaining the best talent** – maintaining employee engagement in the face of a less committed, more flexible workforce.

> ➤ **Late-paying customers** are not just stunting agency growth and harming cashflow, but dramatically

pushing up their debts, by driving many to use overdraft facilities to pay temp. wages and invoice factoring companies.

➤ **The large Managed Service Providers and the Recruitment Process Outsourcers** (MSP/RPO), also have an opportunity, as strategic partners, provided they too learn the new methods of applicant attraction demanded in this social media age.

➤ **Direct-Sourcing Teams** who have the global brands will also have a major part to play. If they can truly leverage their brands to attract staff then they can reduce their organization's dependency on the Recruitment Firms, even dismiss them and perhaps also limit the need to use too many niche agencies.

➤ **Price pressure**, the cost of entry to become a recruiter is low. So anyone can enter the Recruitment industry and call him or herself a recruiter. Often for novices what they tend to do is simply offer low prices due to a misconception that it will mean more business. Of course it doesn't but it does mean the clients want more for less.

Handling the big threats to your business

Is your business built on solid Foundation?

If you were about to build a house for you and your family, you would want to know that it was being built on a firm foundation. Well the same applies to your business!

Let me ask you, have you ever experienced any of these scenarios?

➲ What would the implication be for your business if your number one client were to go bust?

➲ What would be the implication for you and your

business if the government banned your one method for getting business i.e. 'cold calling'?

⮑ What would the implication be for your business if the one finance company that you use were to withhold your finance for 90 days, or worse-case scenario, stop trading with your firm?

⮑ What would be the implication if your one top-billing consultant were to hand in their notice and join your main competitor?

⮑ What if a competitor was to take your one main client from you?

⮑ What would the implication be if the one main job board you use, were to close down tomorrow?

⮑ What would happen to your business if your one main client refused to pay your invoices for 120 days?

Your competitors have experienced all of the above and you could experience the exact same situations too. No warning, absolutely no indication, just there one day and gone the next!

The great marketer Dan Kennedy says, the most dangerous number in any business is the number one. Burying your head in the sand mentality does not serve you. If your competitors have experienced this so can you, it can happen to anyone.

So, the big question is; *"what are you doing to protect yourself and your company from it happening to you?"*

Action Steps

The first step is to identify any scenarios where the number ONE can potentially hurt you.

Here are some examples:

- If you rely on one of anything, you're leaving yourself in an exposed position – you're effectively building your house on a sandy foundation. When the storm comes and the floods rise, the house is going to collapse.

• Identify and eliminate single points of failure in your business.

Conclusion

A question often asked by owners and directors of Recruitment and Search Firms is;

"What's the difference that makes the difference" In other words what's the secret to success in this business?"

In my experience, there is one thing above all others that literally guarantees success. The good news it has nothing to do with intellect, gender, or the colour of your skin. It has all to do with attitude.

You have now read the book, you know what needs to be done to enjoy more success and you know how to influence with elegance and integrity.

So what you should do immediately is focus on what's important. It is really easy to get distracted or fooled in spending time effort and sometimes money on stuff and people that, quite frankly, are neither important nor relevant to the success of your business.

Here is a quick simple and effective method to overcoming the Big Threats facing your business right now:

1. What did you bill/invoice in the last 12 months? (Please no BS about how much 'you could or should have got' as you'll just end up 'shoulding' all over yourself. Just be 100% honest with yourself when you answer that question.)

2. What do you really want to bill/invoice over the next 12 months? It does not need to be some ridiculous figures that would require a team of a 1000 to complete. But it does need to be real and significant.

3. What do you need to have, to achieve that goal?

   • Number of clients you need

   • How many perm. placements per year?

- Average placements value
- Number of contactors/temps. out over 12 months
- Average margins per contractors/temps.
- How many business development meetings most you do each month to achieve goal?
- How many leads/sales inquiries do you need to achieve this goal?

4. What must you do each month to achieve above?

- How many emails to potential clients?
- How many phone calls to potential clients?
- How many connections with potential clients on LinkedIn?
- How many leads will you generate via following:

   Email marketing?

   LinkedIn organic?

   LinkedIn Pay per click?

   Facebook organic?

   Facebook PPC?

   Twitter?

   YouTube?

   Google PPC?

   Remarketing?

   Direct Mail?

   Website ?

Pareto Principle

The 80/20 rule (also known as the 'Pareto Principle') was 'discovered' by Italian sociologist, economist and engineer

Vilfredo Pareto, when he stumbled upon the fact that 80% of the land in Italy was owned by a mere 20% of the population, and that just 20% of his pea plants bore 80% of his pea pods. Then, American management consultant Joseph Juran applied the principle to business on a much wider scale. Here he examined the mysterious 80/20 relationship in multiple aspects of business and from there the "80/20 rule", or "Law" as it's sometimes called, took on a life of its own.

While the exact figures in 80/20 calculations rarely ever match the famous 80/20 ratio, the principle underlying the equation usually proves sound:

✓ The majority of profit comes from a minority of sales.

✓ The majority of work is performed by a minority of employees. Just take a look at your top billing consultant and your underperforming consultants.

✓ The majority of consumer complaints come from a minority of the total customer base (interestingly, here the clients that complain the most also tend to pay the lowest fees).

✓ Knowing this, how can you apply the 80/20 rule to your business in order to boost your productivity, effectiveness and success of your business? Consider it a litmus test you can use to prioritize tasks, examine current systems and pare down your business operations as needed.

✓ The sad fact is most of us spend too much time (80%) doing what has very little value to our business. But what would the implications be for you and your business if you were to spend 80% of your time doing what gives you the results?

✓ So rather being on Facebook looking at what your friends did over the weekend, and you spent 80% doing some of what's in this book, what would the results be?

Here is something to consider

Do you remember the very first time you drove a car, and you had absolutely no idea what to do, even when you were told how to do it? It took every single bit of concentration to get it right.

Now when you drive you think nothing of it, and you can now probably drink a bottle of water and talk to a friend on your mobile (hands-free of course) at the same time. Well, exactly the same applies to what I shared with you!

You see there are four main stages of learning:

1. **Unconscious incompetence**. You're lousy at lead generation for your business, and you don't even know it yet.

2. **Conscious incompetence**. Now you know you're lousy, having just read this book and realized how much business you're missing out on.

3. **Conscious competence.** At this stage you're pretty good, but man, do you have to work at it? This is when you start taking action and doing stuff to get leads.

4. **Unconscious competence.** Now you're good, and you don't even have to think about it. You're now officially ' kicking butt' and generating a TON of leads.

Recruitment Business Owners will often say: *"But I'm too busy to implement this marketing for my business..."* Just think about that statement *"Too busy to grow your business"* – **really...?**

I appreciate that you don't know what exactly to do; I understand the fear and frustration at writing a report, of doing an email to sell your service.

But you're not alone.

To get your free email coaching on how to generate more leads and make more placements simply go to: www.drewcoaching.com/sevendeadlythreats/

The sad fact is too many Staffing/Recruitment Business Owners quit to avoid the frustration or never get started in the first place.

The key to your success is:

TAKING ACTION

> *"The way to get started is to quit talking and begin doing."*
> *Walt Disney, Entrepreneur and Dreamer*

The point is, regardless of what your Staffing/Recruitment Business is like, unless you have targeted and identified those who are ready to buy your Staffing/Recruitment services, you're wasting your time.

Did you know that it's estimated that in your target market right now, between 3% - 10% of your market are what's called ready to buy? They're ready to buy what you offer.

But if they have never heard of you or you're still just cold calling to get business, you're missing out on a ton of business.

To ensure your success you must be communicating with your market so that the 'now buyers' come to you when they're ready to buy.

At the beginning of this book I mentioned some of the big threats you're facing as a Staffing/Recruitment Business Owner. It doesn't matter where in the world you are and what type of Recruitment you do, those threats are there and they're not going to go away anytime soon.

So, I want to help you generate more leads, make more placements and earn more money. Also dispel those out-dated beliefs and myths that the ONLY way to get business is to 'cold call', 'network', or rely on 'word of mouth'. Those methods DO work, but if you're only using them, it's costing you millions in lost revenue, not to mention the lack of security and stress you maybe encountering due the fact you haven't got enough business

There is absolutely no way I could go into enough detail in any of the client/candidate attraction strategies featured in this book, and it should also be noted that I haven't covered every single route to market either. To go into enough depth would be at least another book in itself!

What you have though, are the basic strategies that WILL generate leads and keep you ahead of your competitors.

I'm here to inspire YOU to just take control of YOUR business and YOUR life, because when you do, it takes care of everything in your life including your relationships your love and your self-esteem, so be bold, take action and be relentless in the pursuit of your goals.

I wish you all the best in your Recruiting or Search Firm!

Next steps! (Wait, there's more!)

So, you now have everything you need to get going. However, if you feel you need some extra help, then visit our free resource pages at:

www.drewcoaching.com/sevendeadlythreats/

Not only will you find the specific help sheets listed in the book, but also my *FREE 90 Day acquisition plan*, which will help you achieve more in your recruiting business. Follow it, and you'll see some dramatic results within your business, as well as being leagues ahead of your competitors.

Simply visit:

www.drewcoaching.com/sevendeadlythreats/

...and download it today! Remember, the only way to make a difference is to **TAKE ACTION!** And what better way than to get started than with this plan.

I look forward to seeing you on the site!

About the Author

Terry Edwards, is the worlds leading Recruitment Business Coach, and marketing expert for Recruitment and Search Firms from around the world. He helps them to make more placements, earn more money and work fewer hours

Having written numerous eBooks, including the highly acclaimed *'Why Recruitment Business fail and what to do about it'* and a number of home study courses for the Recruitment industry including *'Rapid Recruitment Profit' Social Media marketing for Search firms.'* He is also the creator of the www.drewcoaching.com/marketingacademy/ which has one of the most successful online marketing sites for Search firms

Over 10,000 Search firm receive his daily business growth emails, and he is also a keynote speaker for many of the industry online events. Very rarely does he open up his private client list to new clients, and the ones he has, very rarely leave!

He is married with three boys, and lives with his wife Sandra in the UK. In the little spare time he has, he is a keen triathlete and spectator of most sport and an avid reader of business books and industry leader biographies.

Acknowledgements

A special thank to my wife Sandra, who has the patience of a Saint and has provided unlimited support, love and guidance, also my eldest son and business partner Drew, who's maturity and wisdom is well beyond his tender years, and Lance and Myles who make me smile everyday.

Over the years I have read many books by some of the leaders of the marketing and self-development industry too many to mention here, but a special thanks to;

Dan Kennedy and all his books, Jon McCulloch, Chris Cardell, Peter Thomson, Anthony Robbins, Brian Tracey, Zig Ziglar, Robert Skrobb, Chet Holmes, Michael Gerber, Stephen Covey and Seth Godin.

Special thanks to Alexa Whitten, (my book writing coach) for not giving up on me. And finally my four sisters and Mum who sadly is no longer with us, but played such a major part of my life and believed in us all.

Thanks Mum...

References

Marianne Williamson, author, from A Return To Love, 1992. Ack C Wilson and J Cooke.

Robert Cialdini, author,   Influence: Science and Practice. 1984. Pearson

Seth Godin, author, Permission Marketing: Strangers into Friends into Customers, 1999, Simon & Schuster Ltd